When You Care Enough

Dedication

This book is dedicated with appreciation to
Hallmark employees and retailers whose pursuit of
quality now spans seven decades.

When You
Care Enough

Joyce C. Hall

with Curtiss Anderson

Hallmark

Contents

Foreword

The fact that I have been associated with Joyce Hall both personally and professionally for almost thirty years does not make it easier for me to transfer to the reader my insights into this complex, fascinating and altogether remarkable man. He has been described as an authentic genius and that he has been. He has been called a dedicated and proud American and that he is. Many see him as the classic prototype of the Horatio Alger tradition of rags to riches in a single lifetime and surely he is that. His life has involved ambition; hard work; tenacity; common sense; an optimistic view of his country, its people and its future; business and personal integrity. But above all, there are two characteristics that have been central to his remarkable achievements — great but disciplined imagination and a deep commitment to the concept of good taste. It was he, among all others, who sensed the potential of a vast increase in social expression by way of the greeting card. But at the same time, he realized that such a development depended on the quality and creative imagination that went into the product. Thus, he searched out the very best and most creative of artists. He insisted on matching the quality of his cards with a comparable quality of their promotion through the Hallmark Hall of Fame, first on radio and then on television. On these basic precepts, an international business empire was built. Thus, "When you care enough to send the very best" was never a tricky slogan but always a proven reality. And among the very best, he has been the best.

DR. FRANKLIN D. MURPHY
January 5, 1979

Introduction: The Hall in Hallmark

For many years Joyce C. Hall has been urged to produce some record of his life and times. As Hallmark Cards grew and prospered, his associates, and even his customers, argued that there was every reason for a book. But he had no enthusiasm for writing his memoirs, and certainly not a formal autobiography. Still, he said, "This idea was put to me as much as anything I'd ever heard. I always suspected people were more interested in some of my friends, for I had the good fortune of knowing some special people."

That he is "special" is an enigma to him but to few others. J. C. Hall is the founder and chairman of the board of Hallmark Cards, Inc., which today employs some ten thousand people, with consumers in over one hundred countries around the world, producing about twelve million greeting cards and related items — *per day*. The Hallmark Hall of Fame is the longest-running and most successful dramatic fare in television history. Joyce Hall has had warm personal friendships with some of the most admired men of our time — Winston S. Churchill, Dwight D. Eisenhower, Harry S. Truman and Walt Disney, to name a few of the most prominent. And he has received countless honors, awards and titles. But it is his grassroots background, literally and figuratively, that gives him the greatest satisfaction — from his beginnings scarcely above the poverty level in a dusty farm community in Nebraska, where he was born in 1891, to Kansas City, Missouri, where he arrived as a teen-ager full of grand illusions and great instincts.

When Joyce Hall was born, Benjamin Harrison was President of the

United States. Sitting Bull was killed the year before, and Wyoming had just become the forty-fourth state. The sinking of the Maine and the Spanish-American War were yet to come. Grover Cleveland became President two years after Joyce Hall's birth. Cleveland was succeeded by McKinley, who was to be assassinated in 1901. Joyce Hall was four years old when the Klondike gold rush overwhelmed the nation. And while a small boy, he learned that his grandfathers had fought in the Civil War on opposite sides at the Battle of Shiloh.

Joyce Hall grew up at a time when a shoot-out at a saloon was not uncommon. (He even witnessed one in which two men were killed.) He rode a stagecoach through the Badlands of South Dakota, and at the age of thirteen sold candy to the notorious Silver Dollar Saloon. He named his first dog Teddy, after the man in the White House. And his first car was a Hupmobile, though his favorite (to this day) was a Stutz Bearcat. As a child he went to Chautauquas and heard William Jennings Bryan orate, then as a young man met the Great Commoner while traveling the railroads as a salesman. Within his memory automobiles replaced the horse and buggy, vaudeville thrived and faded, movies came into their own, the telephone evolved as a household necessity, and in 1908, when he was sixteen, the Wright brothers demonstrated a flying machine that changed the world forever.

Still, to this day, Joyce Hall remains a plainspoken man, retaining the accent of his roots. He seems taller than his six feet, probably because he is lean and erect and projects such innate dignity. He has a prominent proboscis that he is proud of. (In fact, he once observed that the most productive men he hired in the early days seemed inevitably to have large noses.) Accompanying his craggy features is a small thatch of snow-white hair. Norman Rockwell, an old friend (and contributing artist for Hallmark), could have used him as a model for a gentleman farmer of the plains. And he is distinctly out of the old school of the biblical gentle-man. No woman is a "Ms." to J. C. Hall. She is a lady.

His own given name has always been an anathema to him. As a growing boy, being named Joyce was not only embarrassing but challenging as well. His name alone was sufficient grounds for a scuffle with any bully who came along. He finally learned to live with it and even developed a sense of humor about it. His late beloved wife, Elizabeth, was fond of telling a story in this regard that occurred when they were walking their small dachshund named Oscar. (After the death of their male dachshund, who was named Oscar, Elizabeth Hall could not part with the name even for a female dog.) The Halls encountered two young girls, who naturally were attracted to Oscar.

"What's his name?" one of them asked.

Mrs. Hall said, "He's a she, and her name is Oscar."

"That's a funny name for a girl dog," the child replied.

Hall, towering over the girls, leaned down and said,

"And my name is *Joyce*."

Elizabeth Hall was a remarkable woman in her own right. There wasn't anything she couldn't do once she set her mind to it — and as Joyce Hall said, "Just get out of her way." Hall consulted her on any important decision and often reviewed his work with her, whether it was an illustration for a proposed greeting card or a script for a television show. The Hall family — daughters Elizabeth and Barbara and son Donald — were always impressed by their mother's extraordinary stamina. She was an expert equestrienne and taught the entire family to ride the rocky terrain of Colorado where the family had a summer home. Perhaps their youngest daughter, Barbara, best expressed her mother's indomitable spirit. When Barbara was a small child, the family attended a vaudeville show. One of the acts was a female acrobat, who opened by doing a handstand on a chair, rocking back and forth. Then added another chair and another until she was weaving to-and-fro on top of six chairs. At this intensely hushed moment, Barbara stood up and shouted to the audience, "My mommy can do that, too!" It is a story told with great affection by the Hall family.

The entire family is disarmingly unpretentious — and perhaps especially J. C. Hall himself. His uniform at home is a jump suit, which he adopted from his good friend Sir Winston Churchill. Until he was eighty-four years of age, he drove his own car, a 1963 Buick, to his office every day, eschewing Rolls Royces or Cadillacs, not to mention chauffeurs. Not too long ago a young reporter set out to discover just how Joyce Hall felt about being eighty years old and a millionaire. After countless interviews over the years, questions of this sort are of no interest to him so he responded simply: "Lots of people live to be eighty these days — and I don't think anybody needs a million dollars." The reporter asked why he, out of all the people in his home town, had become so successful. "I left, they didn't," Hall replied. The reporter finally had to take an entirely new tack for his story.

These aspects of his life are all quite irrelevant to Joyce Hall. In fact, he is almost totally unaware of his own celebrity. He will speak of notable people with considerable awe (sometimes mistakenly referring to them as "VPIs" instead of "VIPs"). That Churchill, Eisenhower, Truman and Disney were his friends seems to astonish him on reflection, never for a moment realizing that Sir Winston himself made a considerable fuss about his paintings being published by Hallmark. And President Eisenhower was proud to have Hall on the board of the Eisenhower Foundation. President Truman promptly responded to Hall's invitation to speak at an event of his sponsorship. Walt Disney delighted in having his cartoon characters appear on Hallmark products. And all sought and received J. C. Hall's friendship — and he theirs in return.

With his Hall of Fame programs, he admits that he is not just the sponsor but a fan of the various stars who have appeared on the show: Julie Harris, Alfred Lunt and Lynn Fontanne, Mary Martin, Helen Hayes, Peter Ustinov, Judith Anderson, Katharine Cornell, Greer Garson, Maurice Evans. On one of his early programs, Lionel Barrymore surprised him when J. C. Hall rather cautiously asked if he could use some of Barrymore's fine etchings on Christmas cards. Barrymore, grateful for the role, replied, "Hall, I'll do anything you want me to do."

Above all, perhaps, J. C. Hall is a perfectionist. He "cares enough" — some would say "too much," since his relentless drive for quality in his products, including his programs, has exhausted and exasperated a good many people. But the best of them catch his fervor to send the very best. And together with his son, Donald, president of Hallmark Cards since 1966, they have put the company so far out in front of the rest of the industry that most people can't even name another greeting card firm. Hall is fond of pointing out: "That's a pretty good average, having only one son who was so capable of taking over the company and doing such an exceptional job."

People have said that J. C. Hall might have made a success of any business. But he seems to have been drawn to this particular one because of an inborn shyness and an uncompromising decency. So he created an industry — and in so doing created a custom that expresses love, friendship, happiness and sympathy. It is fair to say that Joyce C. Hall made the greeting card industry what it is in America — in the world for that matter. He took an awkward, infant industry and gave it quality. And that is what his life has been all about — his passion for quality. Finally, this pursuit has culminated in the creation of Crown Center in Kansas City, literally a city within a city, which J. C. Hall envisioned and his son expanded even beyond his father's most glowing imaginings.

Joyce C. Hall came out of the birthpangs and growing pains of his beloved land — the big, plain, dazed prairie that had lots of guts and pride but wasn't old enough to have much of a past — just one hell of a future. And the cries from the wilderness were to be somebody, to make something of yourself.

Joyce Hall is an original. His instincts are more often right than wrong, and he is inevitably there first with the best. He originated dozens of concepts for the industry he created. And he has been called "an authentic American genius."

On the pages that follow, Joyce Hall comments informally on his life. He likes to think of these words as shared reminiscences with his family and friends — and everyone who has ever been associated with Hallmark Cards, including those who buy them. He regards his book as neither an autobiography nor a history of Hallmark Cards. That is a task he'd prefer to leave to someone else, if anyone is so inclined. Hall lacks any vanity about posterity. He is simply proud to have been in a business for over sixty-five years that fostered goodwill and has done no harm to anyone.

CURTISS ANDERSON

PART I:
GROWING PAINS

The Gift of Poverty

My earliest memories are of cold winter nights in David City, Nebraska, where I was born in 1891. I slept in an unheated north bedroom with covers piled so high I could barely turn over — and the frost was so thick on the window that when I held a penny to it long enough it would freeze into the glass.

The kitchen was too big to heat, and the water pipe was often frozen. Then we'd have to close off half the kitchen and do our cooking in the dining room, where we had a potbellied stove with one weak leg. It was made to burn wood, but we used coal since there wasn't much wood in this prairie country. One morning, when I was dressing, the stove was red hot, and I put my foot on it to tie my shoe. I jumped back, and the stove fell over. I ran out in zero weather to get help to right it.

Sometimes the snow drifted high enough that we could slide off the roof of our house. We'd also hitch our sleds to the backs of buggies and wagons when the drivers didn't notice. And I remember frost biting through holes in my knitted mittens — and worst of all about winter, the outdoor toilets.

The cold was on my mind so much I'd almost forget that summer would eventually come. The heat was easier to cope with, and we had more food. We managed to have some hens and a few fryers. We had a small vegetable garden and raised raspberries and rhubarb, and we had cherry and plum trees — and once in a while we'd get a catch of catfish.

David City was a conservative county seat in the center of eastern Nebraska, about sixty miles west of Omaha. The population was eighteen hundred then, and it's about the same now. People were second or third generation Americans, except for a Bohemian settlement east of town. It was strictly a farm community that raised corn and wheat. Most farmers had a couple of milk cows, a flock of chickens, some turkeys, hogs and maybe a few sheep. I would drive cows to pasture to earn a little bucket of skimmed milk. The milk was let down into a well for about fifteen feet so it would stay cold. Butter was cheap, but we didn't always have it, especially in winter. After eating cornbread without butter for a number of days, we'd scare up a dime for a pound of butter that was scooped out of a community tub. In hot weather there was a block of ice in it.

When food was scarce in our house, somehow my mother wouldn't have an appetite. And if the night got cold, I would wake up with another blanket. She was a wonderful mother who said very little, but what she said she meant. She was not very strong and was often ill. She wasn't always physically able to take care of us; so I learned to cook, and that's no handicap to any boy. She was told she wouldn't live very long, but she said, "Yes, I will. I'll see my children raised." And she did.

I had two brothers, Rollie, who was nine years older than I, and Bill, seven years older. My sister, Marie, was four years younger. My mother's first child died in infancy. None of us were much alike in appearance. My brothers were small like my mother. I took after my father and sprouted to six feet. My hair was almost black, Rollie's was brown and Bill's almost blond.

As a child it troubled me more than I can say that I was named Joyce and my brothers had such familiar names as Rollie and William. My mother named me after a Methodist bishop from Minneapolis (Bishop Isaac W. Joyce) who happened to be in David City the day I was born. I was fully grown before I wasn't ashamed of my name. I did not pass it on to my own son as a first name, only as a middle name.

Neither Rollie nor I had a middle name (Bill's was Finch), but Rollie felt we should. He had a teacher named Beatrice whom he particularly favored; so he took Beatrice as his middle name. I thought I should follow his example in this as I had in many other things. I decided my middle name should be Burlington — I don't remember why, but I suspect it was because the Chicago, Burlington and Quincy was one of the three railroads that went through David City.

4

I bought a rubber stamp, set the letters of my chosen name, and in all my school books, I neatly printed: JOYCE BURLINGTON HALL. When Rollie came across this, he said, "That name's no good. I'll give you a better one." He thought about it for some time, then he settled on Clyde. I still preferred Burlington, but I was too young to fight for it. Also, I not only looked up to Rollie as a big brother, but he was like a father to all of us. He was all wool and a yard wide. I especially remember his many small kindnesses when I was a child. He'd come home at night from the store where he worked and bring me a special treat, like a chocolate bear that cost a penny.

My father, George Nelson Hall, had a lot of ability, but there wasn't much chance to use it in a small farming community. Before I was born, he ran a little hardware store in Brainard, Nebraska, a town of about five hundred. He couldn't have done very well since he gave up the store and moved to David City. I might have gotten a little retailing in my blood from my father. He was an inventor of sorts, too, and I remember he had a patent on one of his inventions, a wire fly swatter.

Mainly, I remember my father as an itinerant preacher. He would travel to various Methodist churches and be gone for as long as six months. We weren't poor because my father couldn't make a living — we were poor because he let us be. Although he always seemed to have some money himself, he sent very little to us. He told my mother that she needn't worry — "the Lord would provide." I found out then that it was a good idea to give the Lord a little help. When I was seven years old, my father left home for good. We never really knew why.

One of the things that gave me an extra drive to succeed was a good appetite. I wanted to eat regularly — and I had seen stretches when I didn't. Poverty for me was a tremendous spur. It actually gave me an advantage over a lot of folks when I was starting out.

My grandparents on my father's side were important people in my life. My grandmother — actually she was my grandfather's second wife — was a little bit of an Irishwoman. At least I think of her as Irish, I guess because she was such a lively woman. She was a great gardener. She could spade more ground in an hour than any man who has ever worked for me, and she could raise finer flowers outdoors than most people can in a greenhouse. She was a wonderful cook, too. On the way home from school, she'd give me homemade graham bread, hot out of the oven, with butter and a little sugar on it.

Grandfather Hall was a retired farmer by the time I was born. He was not a very talkative man, but he was a wonderful grandfather. He gave me a penny once in a while, and he called me "Snoozer." He would sit all afternoon on the porch, watching the neighbors go by and nodding a greeting.

He was an active prohibitionist. After one election he somehow got a list of all the men in town who had voted for a local liquor option. He had the list printed on handbills, which he had me peddle to every house in David City. The next day he and I were sitting on some steps in the town square when the saloon owner came up to him. He called my grandfather every nasty name I had ever heard and a lot I hadn't. For about five minutes grandfather ignored him. Then he jumped up, grabbed him by the shirt and said, "You say one more word and I'll crush your backbone into jelly." There was nothing more said.

He had breakfast at six, dinner at noon and supper at six. And he always had an apple at eight before he went to bed. He was never sick a day in his life that I remember. He was in his seventies when one morning he was found dead in his bed.

My other grandparents lived in Kentucky, although my mother had grown up in Hannibal, Missouri, about the time of Samuel L. Clemens (or Mark Twain). Her maiden name was Nancy Dudley Houston; her great uncle was Sam Houston. She taught school a few years before she married my father. She had a stepfather, my grandmother's second husband, and occasionally they visited us. One day in talking, we discovered that my two grandfathers had fought on opposite sides in the Battle of Shiloh.

We had a young couple living with us for a short time. They rented our parlor as their living quarters. They were just out of college from Omaha and started a bowling alley in town. It was the first time I had ever heard of bowling. They had a music box, which was also new to me. They were very kind, and I learned a great deal from them. It was the first time that educated and refined people had ever paid any attention to me.

In David City at the turn of the century, we went to school because we had to. Not much reason was ever given why we should take it seriously. We lived for the end of the school year when we could go barefoot, swim in the pond and play baseball and "Run, Sheep, Run." The girls and smaller boys would play "Pussy Wants a Corner" and "Hide and Go Seek."

We'd walk to the South Ward School in sunshine or snow. It never occurred to anyone not to walk, no matter what the weather was like or the distance. Two things stick in my mind about the sanitary conditions of that school — the outdoor toilets and the water we'd drink from a common bucket. We'd take a dipper full then throw the water we didn't drink back into the bucket.

There was no homework in grade school and not much in high school. One hundred was a perfect grade and sixty passing. I got good grades in history and geography. In other subjects I got just above sixty. I was taught to read slowly, pronouncing every syllable. As the years passed I learned to read faster by myself.

Two classmates I especially remember were Lucy Hughes and Lucille Downing. Lucy was a little black-haired girl who sat in front of me. She had braids down her back, and I stuck them in the inkwell one morning. I had to sit in front of the class with my feet straight out on the floor until noon. Lucille Downing was a pretty little blond. I would chase her home from school with the idea that if I caught her I got to kiss her. But the closer I got to her, the shorter of breath I was — so I never caught her. The truth is, I was afraid to catch her because I was afraid to kiss her.

I didn't finish high school with my class because my brothers and I had to take jobs to support the family. But some fifty-five years later I returned to David City to receive an honorary high-school diploma, graduating with the class of 1962. A reporter for the David City newspaper interviewed me and wrote: "The class of 1962 has high hopes for member Joyce C. Hall."

Two great events during the summer were the Fourth of July and the Chautauquas. For a whole week David City was on the Chautauqua circuit. Families would come from towns and farms all around and stay the week. A big tent went up in the park, and there would be entertainment all day and into the night — military bands, choruses, quartets, comedians, trained dogs. And there'd be speeches, too — speakers supporting prohibition, ministers preaching against sin, Burton Holmes showing his travel slides, Robert La Follette and William Jennings Bryan talking politics.

Grandmother Wilson

Grandfather Hall

Grandfather Hall in front of first livery barn in David City, Nebraska

Nancy Dudley Hall, circa 1895

Rollie B. Hall, circa 1900

Joyce Hall, circa 1892

The Fourth of July was almost as exciting. The celebration would start with fireworks before daylight. And there was no limit then to the size of fireworks that could be sold. Fires would always get started, and the rougher element in town would get drunk. There were plenty of accidents, and sometimes serious ones. I saw a little girl get her finger shot off and a boy lose an eye. And there was a fellow standing in the street with a big firecracker in his hip pocket. Somebody lit it.

My first real job was working on a farm when I was eight years old. I expected to plow, raise corn, drive cattle, cut hay — and even ride a horse. But the lady of the house was expecting a baby, and I became the nurse and kitchen maid. So, I learned more about cooking. Her husband would leave at daylight for the field, and later I would take him something to eat and a jug of cold well water.

Times were tough. They had plenty of green beans in the garden, but nothing else, and plenty of bacon in the smokehouse, but nothing else; so we usually had green beans and smoked bacon to eat. It was a drought year, and I learned a great thing that summer — the joy of rain after a long dry spell. There can be no finer thrill — dressed in a thin shirt or none at all — than to just stand in the grass and feel the rain coming down.

From then on I always had some job. When the circus came to town and on Sundays at the ball park, I would sell lemonade. You could make a whole tub of lemonade with the juice of one lemon, a little bit of citric acid and about twenty-five cents worth of sugar. The ball players played mostly for fun, plus a few dollars and a cold beer. But some of them went on to the major leagues, such as Wahoo Sam Crawford, Grover Cleveland Alexander and Dazzy Vance.

If you got up and out by dawn, you could usually get a job — with payment being a free ticket — at the circus. I set up stakes for the tents, carried water and fed the animals. And, like every kid, I guess I wanted to join the circus, too. The first VIP I ever met was one of the Ringling brothers. He came to our house by mistake, looking for my grandfather to buy hay for the circus horses.

My first business ventures all seem to have involved food. Three railroads came through David City, and there was no food service on the trains. I made sandwiches at home to sell to the passengers.

My next venture was in horseradish with a fellow named Earl Beatch, who was twice my age. We had labels made to read "L. E. Beatch and Company, Strictly Pure Horseradish." But instead of "Strictly Pure," the labels read "Sticky Pure," and we couldn't afford to print new ones. I was the "and company." I grew the horseradish, dug it, grated it on a small hand grater (which was a rough job with no protection for your eyes) and bottled it. Beatch sold it for ten cents a bottle. There were no profits — to me anyway. I got over my pride in being a businessman fast when I didn't get a cent out of it.

But I was learning, and my early ambition may have been sparked partly by the drummers, or traveling salesmen, who'd come to town. The leading hotel (there were only two, but I guess you could call the Perkins "the leading one") was on a corner of the courthouse square, with room for a few trees and easy chairs. In good weather the drummers would sit around and swap yarns. I used to listen. They did give a small boy ambition to get out into the world, although I didn't realize then that their success stories were a bit exaggerated.

When I was nine years old I became a drummer of sorts myself. A woman representing the California Perfume Company came to town to find an agent to sell door-to-door. She called on my mother to offer her the job, but mother wasn't strong enough. In fact, by then she was practically an invalid, and she wouldn't have had the five dollars to buy the sample case needed for selling anyway.

When I heard about it, I raced over to see my grandfather. He listened carefully to my story without saying a word. Then he got out his wallet and gave me five dollars. I approached the woman about being the agent and had to sell pretty hard. She said, "Well, I haven't got one here anyway, and I might as well let you try it." So I got the job because no one else in town wanted it.

One of the products was cosmetics, and the only women who used them (and had any money) were those politely called "the women across the river in the white cottage" — but that was out of bounds for me. Besides cosmetics, I sold lemon extract, lilac cologne, soap and tooth powder. It took a lot of selling after school and on Saturdays. I didn't know anything about credit, but I learned. If a lady said, "Leave the perfume and I'll pay you next Monday," I thought she'd do just that. But I soon found out what "poor credit risk" means. I got a forty percent commission on what I sold and turned everything over to my mother.

THE DRUMMER'S LATEST YARN.

THE DRUMMER'S LATEST YARN.

A happy-go-lucky individual is the commercial traveler. He carries the burden of his house upon his shoulders; skirmishes the country for traffic, and keeps the wolf from the governor's door. He has a keen scent for trade and a sweet tooth for a good story.

Is sometimes known as a missionary, sent out to convert the untutored trader; the drummer, to rattle up trade and make a noise for the house. He is of a romantic turn, is fond of cheerful company, loves a congenial spirit, and regards a sprightly maiden's chatter as better than lost time.

His talent for story telling is marvelous, and crisp, bright, pointed ones are found in his stock, *if in the market.*

No Mouldy Chestnuts for the Drummer.

Recently a very gifted member of the fraternity told a particularly good story to a very appreciative man coming up the Lake Shore road. His laughter, very hearty at first, became hysterical and could not be stopped; he struggled, strangled and died in the car.

While sudden takings off are melancholy, it was a comfort to the immediate friends that he died happy.

The drummer has not dared tell that story since.

The artist, A. M. Willard, of Cleveland, was a passenger on the train, and his sketch taken on the spot may be relied on.

12

An early example of good housekeeping, L.W. Snow's store

Union Pacific dining car, circa 1900

It was a good, early business experience for me and evidently for the California Perfume Company. Sometime later the company changed its name — to Avon Products.

My brothers worked in odd jobs, too. They were about fifteen and seventeen years old when a salesman named L. W. Snow came to town and opened a millinery and notions store. They worked in the store after school and on Saturdays. Mr. Snow traveled, selling candy, while his wife ran the store. He had quite an effect on our lives because he later took my brothers with him to Columbus, Nebraska, before they'd finished school. He had bought a bookstore there and, under Mrs. Snow's supervision, had my brothers run it while they lived with the Snows.

Columbus was bigger than David City and sort of magical to me. I hadn't seen much to compare with the store before either, and I thought it was great. It was the only bookstore in town, and it also carried magazines, candy, cigars and a few other things. Mr. Snow was a good merchant. He'd replace poor-selling products promptly with something better. He believed in good housekeeping, too. He kept the candy case full, the glass sparkling and the floor swept.

I would go to Columbus to sell fireworks for Mr. Snow the week before the Fourth of July, and I'd get excused from school a week early to help with the Christmas rush. Another one of my jobs was to go to the Union Pacific station a couple of blocks from the store and pick up newspapers that came in from Omaha and Lincoln. I'd pass the Pullman and dining cars on the Union Pacific's main line trains to the West Coast and look at the well-dressed people sitting at the tables. Some of them would have big baked potatoes with as many as three pieces of butter. My mouth would water. I got the idea then that if I ever made any money, every day I would have a baked potato with three pieces of butter.

Post Cards, Popcorn and Sweeping Compound

In 1902 Rollie and Bill went in with a distributing agent for the *Nebraska State Journal*, W. S. Jay, to buy a bookstore in Norfolk, Nebraska, about sixty miles north of David City. When school was out in the spring, I went up to Norfolk to work in the store. It wasn't long before the entire family moved to Norfolk, leaving David City for good. At last we were out of extreme poverty, largely because of Rollie and Bill.

There was quite a difference between the two towns. Norfolk was about twice the size of David City. It was a railroad center with branch lines of the Chicago and North Western and the Union Pacific. This not only made Norfolk a much more progressive town but also a tough pioneering community.

The day I left David City by train, a man boarded a few stations before Norfolk. It was clear he hadn't neglected his thirst. He made a few loud remarks that he thought were funny, but there was something about him that was frightening. I couldn't take my eyes off him. It wasn't uncommon in those days to carry a gun, but shooting it was another matter. Suddenly he pulled a revolver from his hip pocket and took three shots right down the aisle. As we all ducked behind our seats, I could almost feel the bullets whizzing over my head.

A young brakeman heard the commotion from the vestibule and came rushing in. Before the drunk had a chance to turn around, the brakeman pulled a gun. I thought he was going to shoot him right there. Instead, he hit him over the head with the butt. The drunk slept the rest of the way to Norfolk, where the town marshal had been telegraphed and was waiting for the train.

Bill was to have met me at the station, but he wasn't there. It was only two or three blocks to the store; so I set out walking. On the way I saw a big crowd in front of the barbershop, where Bill had been detained. The wooden sidewalks were being replaced by concrete, and the sand

15

had been leveled for pouring cement the next day. The barbershop porter had gotten into an argument with an equally husky townsman. Both were stripped to the waist and fighting it out in the sand. For about forty-five minutes, with a couple of interruptions by self-appointed referees, the two of them slammed away at each other until their eyes were practically closed. By the time they both looked like a couple of raw beefsteaks, the police force in its entirety, a day marshal and a night marshal, stopped the fight.

That was not the worst fight I was to see in Norfolk. There was a lot of gambling in town, and two of the regulars were bitter enemies. I still remember their names — Charlie Dugan, a young man, and Lee Bailey, who was about sixty-five. One afternoon Dugan and a few other men, including the mayor, were playing poker in the Buffet Saloon. Bailey was standing nearby when Dugan made insulting remarks about him. Bailey threatened him with a gun. Dugan left, vowing he'd return with a gun himself; Bailey said he'd be waiting.

Sometime later Dugan came down the street with a crowd following him. The saloon was across the street and a few doors to the left of our store. I followed the crowd, thinking I could run back to the store if a customer arrived. I climbed an awning bar on the window of the saloon and had a peephole just big enough to see what was going on. Dugan walked in; he and Bailey drew their guns. I was paralyzed. Dugan shot first and Bailey fell, dropping his gun to the floor. He raised himself up on one elbow and retrieved his gun even though Dugan kept shooting. Bailey managed to get in a shot or two, and Dugan collapsed. Two other men in the saloon were wounded in the crossfire.

Dugan was helped into an automobile belonging to a doctor. There was no ambulance in Norfolk then. Bailey lay stretched out on the floor with what looked like the whole town gathered around him. He was dead — and by the next morning so was Dugan.

About a year later a man named Valley B. Nethaway, a champion marksman, went down to the afternoon train carrying a shotgun and a revolver. His wife was on board going to the county seat to attend a hearing on her petition for a divorce. Just as the train left, Nethaway jumped on, entered the passenger car and told everybody to sit still. He said he was not going to hurt or rob anyone; he was just going to shoot his wife. "Woman, prepare yourself to die," he shouted. People screamed and jumped for cover. A few managed to leap out the windows of the moving train. He emptied both barrels of the shotgun into his wife.

The train screeched to a halt, and Nethaway ran. He got as far as the office of a grain company, where he told the man who ran the grain elevator that he was going to kill himself. The man tried to talk Nethaway out of committing suicide, but it was no use. So he asked him if he wouldn't at least go into one of the buildings to do it rather than right in his office. Nethaway agreed, went into the elevator and shot himself through the head with his revolver.

My salary at the bookstore was eighteen dollars a month, which was a lot to me. It was even enough to save a little. During school months I'd get to the store about seven in the morning to sweep and dust, then return at noon so Bill could go to lunch. After school I worked until supper at six, then immediately returned until closing at ten. It was exciting to me with all the bright new books and magazines on display. I enjoyed reading them and studying the ads. In fact, my strong interest in advertising probably began there.

American Magazine was my favorite, especially its stories on outstanding men in the public eye. Other popular magazines of the day were *Munsey's Weekly, Harper's, Leslie's Weekly, Ladies' Home Journal, Literary Digest, Woman's Home Companion* and *The Saturday Evening Post. Everybody's Magazine* was not particularly popular until it published Thomas Lawson's "Frenzied Finance;" then sales in our store jumped from six to eight copies a month to ten times as many.

As winter came, with less activity in the store, I had more time to read the best-selling books of the day. There is a marked difference between best sellers then and now. Few from that period would sell today, and many of the current best sellers wouldn't even have been accepted in the mail, much less published. Some of my favorite writers were Harold MacGrath, who wrote a popular novel called *"The Man on the Box;"* Mark Twain; Zane Grey; Booth Tarkington; Harold Bell Wright; and Winston Churchill. (Many years later, I came to know Winston Churchill, the great English statesman. He told me that he had written the writer of the same name, asking him if he would consider changing his name. The writer replied angrily that he had made his own reputation and was not about to change his name.)

The big sellers for children were the Horatio Alger books, *Little*

Women, Five Little Peppers and How They Grew, Mrs. Wiggs of the Cabbage Patch and *Black Beauty*. Books of poetry and fantasy illustrated by Charles Dana Gibson, James Montgomery Flagg and Howard Chandler Christy also sold well — some for as much as five dollars a copy, an enormous price then.

We did a fair book business, and magazines sold well. But, unfortunately, the store had a lot of slow-moving, old merchandise, particularly glassware and wallpaper, which really got Rollie's goat. He said, "No one would accept this stuff as a gift." The cigar counter was easily the busiest part. We'd play dice poker with customers, who could win free cigars — or pay double. We came out about even, but we sold more cigars this way than we would have otherwise. This was a common sales method in such communities. Today, even if it were allowed, the time it would take would make it unprofitable.

It was perfectly respectable to smoke cigars and pipes — or even chew tobacco or snuff. Meerschaum (white clay) pipes were the most expensive. Anyone who smoked a corncob pipe was considered a hick. Meerschaums turned various shades of brown as they were smoked, and it was considered very smart to polish the bowl on your nose. But a man who smoked cigarettes was considered a punk. And if he smoked tailor-made ones, he simply wasn't welcome in this part of the country. Handmade cigarettes, usually rolled with Duke's Mixture or Bull Durham, were more acceptable. Still, any cigarette then was called a "coffin nail." At the time we didn't know how accurate that was.

We also had a good candy business, especially hand-dipped chocolates. One of my jobs was to keep the glass plates full. Bulk orders sold for forty cents a pound and boxes for fifty. One customer, William Werner, a German who ran a saloon, would come by every Saturday night about nine o'clock and buy five dollars' worth of bulk chocolates. He had three daughters, who turned out to be very attractive in spite of eating all that candy.

In those days it wasn't easy to control the problem of rats. We'd hear some scratching and immediately go on the attack. One blizzardy winter night I heard whining and scratching that sounded like a rat somewhere in the front of the store. In fact, the sounds seemed to come straight from the front door — and sometimes a rat did come right in off the street.

I grabbed a broom, ready to attack, and pushed open the door.

Standing there, with the saddest little face, was a puppy that couldn't have been more than a couple of months old. He looked like a dachshund, but when I came across a picture of him recently, I realized he was probably more beagle than anything else.

He bounced in the door, delighted to see me. Not having a dog, I was just as delighted to see him. He looked as if he hadn't eaten for some time; so I got some scraps from a restaurant nearby. The pup was just the right size to fit into the sleeve of my coat, and I bundled him up for the long walk home. My mother was not too happy to see him, but when she finally picked him up and cuddled him, I knew I had a dog. He became my constant companion. I named him Teddy. Theodore Roosevelt was President then, and a large percentage of dogs — and a good many children — were named Teddy.

By this time we had a comfortable, two-story house with central heating and an inside bathroom. Rollie was on the road most of the time selling candy, and both he and Bill had respectable incomes. I took on extra jobs, such as selling newspapers on Saturday night. We were able to save money largely because we were used to not spending any.

Everybody came out Saturday night, usually walking or by horse and buggy. The first automobile in town was a Jackson owned by a banker. He took me on a Sunday afternoon drive, which was the first time I had ever ridden in an automobile. That experience added one more thing to my list of what I wanted when I got rich.

We didn't get the newspapers to the store until about eight o'clock, but the crowd started gathering by seven, marching up and down the street and generally having a good time. A few of the country's largest newspapers had started comic sections with their Sunday editions, and the nearest one was the *Chicago American*. We'd get as many as four hundred copies, and they'd go almost immediately. People made a big event of their Saturday-night "funny papers." There were eight comics, and I remember most of them: Happy Hooligan, Buster Brown, the Katzenjammer Kids, Alfonse and Gatson, Her Name Was Maude, Lady Bountiful.

The papers arrived at the Norfolk junction about a mile from downtown, and it took a couple of trips by bicycle to get all four hundred to the store. This is when I found out more about the problem of being a boy named Joyce moving into a new town. There was a tough young

Joyce, Marie and Rollie Hall in front of Norfolk bookstore

Joyce Hall, age eleven, far left, with group at boarding house

Joyce Hall, at left, on boating excursion on the North Fork River

*At age twelve with Marie Tracy,
the prettiest girl in the class*

Teddy, 1902

fellow named Stub Turlock, about my age, thirteen or fourteen, who lived along the route. He took particular delight in giving me trouble getting the papers uptown, like jumping out from behind a tree and pushing my load over. This was only the beginning of my difficulties with him.

When I went to school that fall, the first weeks were anything but easy. I soon found out that I was going to have to whip a few fellows before I would have any standing in Norfolk. Finally, one boy jumped me going home from school. I gave him a beating. From then on he was a friend, but I still had few others.

Stub was the ringleader and everyone was afraid of him, including me. Then one Saturday I was handling the store alone. About noon I ran to the restaurant a few doors away to get a sandwich to bring back to the store. Stub was sitting on some steps, and as I passed, he tripped me. I fell flat on my face. It shook me up, but it didn't knock me out. I climbed onto him before he could get off the steps and learned then that he was just a bully who was mostly talk. We never became friends, but he gave me no further trouble.

Rollie only spent about one weekend a month at home; the rest of the time he traveled through western Nebraska, Wyoming and the Black Hills of South Dakota selling candy for an Omaha factory. During my second summer in Norfolk, in 1903, Rollie took me along on my first trip through that territory. I was only twelve, and it was one of the great adventures of my life. He introduced me to his customers so that the following summer I could handle his territory while he took a month's vacation, the first one in his life.

Rollie would skip one or two towns en route, then work the next town where we got off. Then he'd catch a train back to the towns we had missed. At first I couldn't understand this, but he said it was an important part of working a small-town territory. In each town he had only one account, and he would be able to sell what he could in half an hour or so. If he took just the one passenger train and one freight train that came along each day, he would get in only two towns. Most drummers would do just that. They were satisfied just to take the towns as they came. Of course, some had big lines of merchandise that took half a day to show, but that wasn't the case with candy. What I learned from Rollie about making the best use of time proved valuable to me the rest of my life.

Not knowing what to expect in this part of the country, I took a .22 revolver along. On one forty-mile stretch we got a ride with a mailman in a buckboard (an uncovered heavy buggy), and we spotted a bevy of prairie chickens. He said it was too bad we didn't have a gun. That's when I pulled the .22 out of my bag. Normally I couldn't hit the broad side of a barn, but I somehow managed to get a bird. When I brought it back to the buckboard, the mailman said, "That's pretty good shooting. Too bad I'm the game warden." He pulled back his coat to show me his badge. But he not only didn't take any official action, he joined us for a prairie chicken dinner. Rollie gave me a tongue-lashing for having the gun, but he let me keep it.

We traveled through the Badlands to the Pine Ridge Indian Reservation. Rollie always got a good order here since no other candy man ever showed up. While it was illegal to sell liquor to Indians, there was no law against selling lemon extract, but it must have had a lot of alcohol, because it had the same effect. The drummer who handled it sold it by the wagonload. The sides of the road were so littered with empty bottles that you could hardly see the ground. The bottles had sunken sides to make them look larger and sold for about ten cents each or twelve for a dollar. The sad thing was that it took a good part of the Indians' government allowance to buy the extract.

It was also sad to see how the Indians had to live on the reservation. People said they were lazy and didn't want to farm — and maybe they were right. But the Indians' background made hunting much more appealing than farming. And anyone who has been to the Badlands knows what good-for-nothing country it is. On the Pine Ridge Reservation they probably couldn't even raise a cactus plant. The Sioux here originally had been much farther east. But I suppose some Yankee trader had swapped the Indians this land for some fertile Ohio Valley farmland.

Like most boys my age, Indians fascinated me. However, I had never met any until this trip. When we got to Chadron, Nebraska, I saw a few Indians around town. Then we went to the drugstore, a good account of Rollie's, and I got to talking about Indians to the owner's son, Henry Maika, who was about my age. He asked if I'd like to ride a bicycle to the Indian camp. It was an exciting idea, but it made the back of my scalp uncomfortable.

To my twelve-year-old eyes, there must have been three thousand or more Indians in the camp. Henry was used to being around them, and in a mixture of English and Sioux, he seemed to converse with no problem. There were lines strung between trees along one side of the camp with some kind of meat hanging to dry in the sun. I wondered what it was, and Henry enlightened me — dog meat. Nothing was wasted; it hung out all day, covered with flies. The place didn't smell like a rose garden. There were also one-gallon tin cans in which the Indians cooked their food. It didn't look like much of a banquet. I was amazed at how little they required aside from the clothes on their backs. There was practically nothing in the wigwams except buffalo robes. I wondered how safe we'd be after dark, but that didn't bother Henry; so I acted as if it didn't bother me either.

The following summer I went to Omaha with Rollie to get his candy samples in order. He bought me my first pair of long pants. He wanted to make a little more of a man out of me to take over his territory. Fortunately, most of Rollie's customers had become his good friends, and they would give me an order. A few even gave me extra orders, either to make me feel good or to have something to kid Rollie about.

The trip included Lander, Wyoming, which was still a wild cow town. I stayed in a one-story hotel on the main street, where all the stores and saloons were located. The sidewalk was about three feet off the ground under a corrugated metal roof so that wagons could back up to the stores to be easily loaded. I was in a front room right on the walk. About midnight a few cowpunchers got drunk and rode up and down the wooden walk, shooting their six-shooters through the roof. In spite of my long pants, I was not feeling very brave.

The Black Hills territory included the town of Lead, South Dakota, where the Hearst family owned what I believe was the biggest gold mine in operation — the Homestake. Deadwood was just a few miles away with the notorious Silver Dollar Saloon, which had been open night and day for a good many years. In fact, it was said that the key to the front door had never been used. The floor of the saloon was decorated with silver dollars set in tile. I had to call there because there was a lunch counter in the back of the saloon that sold quite a lot of candy.

The Deadwood Stagecoach, which was always written up by *Wild*

West Weeklies, was perhaps the most famous at that time. It ran to Spearfish and Belle Fourche, South Dakota. This was the territory of Deadeye Dick, Calamity Jane and Wild Bill Hickok, and there were still plenty of similar characters around. I rode with a couple of them the day I took the coach and couldn't take my eyes off them, expecting something to happen at any moment. It was exciting to see this untamed territory, but it was also a relief to leave.

Traveling back and forth on Rollie's territory, I got to know many other drummers on the route. Because I was just seventeen, some of them would take me under their wings — and even introduce me to their dealers and urge them to buy my line. However, one drummer with good intentions gave me some bad advice, and I didn't know any better at the time. He told me to double an order I had for candy from a particularly conservative dealer. Well, it worked — and I was proud to have sold twice as much as the man had ordered. But the second time I tried it with another dealer, the man wrote to Rollie complaining — and the practice ended abruptly. Rollie's training held me in good stead — to play it honest with his dealers and work around the clock. I was convinced that salesmanship made the world go round, and there was little doubt in my mind then that my future was in selling.

Back then conductors would even hold trains for salesmen, finally blowing a whistle to give them five minutes to finish their calls. In return the drummers would throw a few dollars into a kitty for the conductor. Another practice was to pay the conductor half the fare of the ticket in cash, which he pocketed. I didn't know about this, so when I presented a fully paid ticket to one conductor, he replied, "I can't even buy baby shoes with that." Auditors were put on trains to discourage these practices; then a few lines hired private detectives to watch the conductors and the auditors.

There was always a party atmosphere on the trains with the jovial, hard-working drummers swapping yarns and shooting dice. And there were plenty of cigars and a bottle or two to pass around. This was quite an atmosphere for a young man, traveling in such adult company — and most of all, being accepted.

When I got back to Norfolk, Rollie rewarded me with a hunting-case pocket watch for working his territory. It was a Howard watch worth about forty-five dollars, extremely expensive for that time. It still runs, and I cherish it to this day.

By fall the Rosebud Indian Reservation was opened for settlement, and a couple of passenger trains were to come through Norfolk every night for a week taking settlers to the little town of Bonesteel, South Dakota, where there was a lottery to draw for sites. The first night they came through, I popped and sacked all the popcorn I could carry and went down to meet the train. I sold out in a few minutes and had enough time before the second train arrived to repeat the process.

But I thought I could do even better. So the next night I had someone help me push the popcorn wagon down to the junction on the main line a mile away. I popped corn as fast as it would pop and had a ton of it on hand by the time the first train arrived. This went on for five or six nights. On the best night I sold more than eighty dollars worth at five cents a bag. Popcorn was practically all profit. A big sack of corn on ears could be bought at the feed store for twenty-five cents, and one pound of butter took care of a lot of bags of popcorn. This was the main source of my first operating capital: I had saved $180.

One evening in 1905 when I was alone in the store, a snappy-looking young man in a derby hat walked in. His visit turned out to be a milestone in my life, although I certainly didn't realize it then. Many times since, I've wondered where I'd be and what I'd be doing if he hadn't stopped in our store that night.

When told that the proprietor was not expected until some time later, he hung around — and passed the time talking to me. He was a representative of one of the larger New York importers of illustrated post cards. The cards were vivid, German-type lithography, and larger than standard cards today. The post card craze was at its peak. Almost everybody had an album or two to keep the cards people sent. Most of them had messages, such as birthday greetings, and a few said nothing at all.

The dapper gentleman had come all the way from Chicago to Fremont, Nebraska, about sixty miles from us, to see someone who had expressed an interest in wholesaling post cards. They had some misunderstanding and parted poor friends; so he continued on to Norfolk. He explained how successful some wholesalers had been in small towns like ours. I asked how much money it would take. He said the deal in Fremont would have amounted to an inventory of about one thousand dollars worth of post cards for a start.

Rollie was out of town working his territory, but I kept the store open late hoping Bill would show up. Finally, the man said he'd return in the morning. I went home to wait for Bill. I told him I would put up my $180, and if he and Rollie matched it, we'd have $540, perhaps enough to get us started. Bill just didn't take the post card business — or me — very seriously.

The next morning the man talked to Bill. Being a better salesman than I, in a couple of hours he convinced Bill that we should go into the post card business on a wholesale level. We picked out the cards that would make up our first order for a firm that I had already named the Norfolk Post Card Company.

We counted Rollie in without even consulting him. The man explained that we could get salesmen to handle post cards as a sideline, and we figured Rollie would do just that. We fixed up a sample line of cards, and Rollie started to get orders. It took some doing, but I convinced my brothers that I could sell cards, too — after school on Fridays and in two or three more towns on Saturdays.

We also approached every salesman who came to the store about selling our line of post cards in whatever territory he was working. At first only a few of them sold enough cards to pay for making up the sample line. But gradually we had about half a dozen drummers doing reasonably well.

Bill was named president, although I don't believe we ever had an election. I sorted the cards and filled the orders; Bill made out the invoices. Since none of us drew a salary and there was no overhead, we began making a small profit.

As soon as school was out, I made one- and two-week trips through Nebraska and South Dakota. On one excursion I met a grocery drummer who not only knew all the merchants in the towns but every angle possible in covering them. He asked if I had ever worked the Oconee Turnaround, then explained that it was a freight train that left Scribner, Nebraska, early in the morning and went through about eight towns to the village of Oconee.

It was on the Oconee Turnaround that I ran into a man from Cedar Rapids, Iowa, who was selling a new product called sweeping compound. Most stores then had pine floors, and few streets were paved; so customers tracked in a lot of dirt. Sweeping the floor was a messy

The Deadwood Stage, 1904

Pine Ridge Indian Reservation around the turn of the century

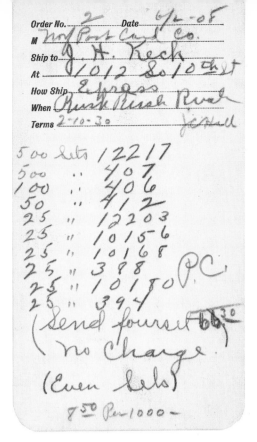

Joyce at age eleven, top right

Rollie, the salesman, around 1906

A Happy Christmas to you!

A merry Christmas

Best Wishes for Christmas

To
From
A Merry Christmas

This is just to say
I am thinking of you to-day

Why DON'T You Write?

To the Valentine of my choice

CHOOSE YOUR LOVE AND THEN LOVE YOUR CHOICE.

MARY·ELEANOR·GEORGE

A Merry Christmas

Thanksgiving Greetings.

Easter Greetings

Easter Joys.

FOOLISH QUESTIONS

"Mowing the grass?"
"Naw!
Peelin' Pertaters
with a buzz saw."

? ? ? ? ? ? ? ?

COPYRIGHT 1909 BY H.A. WATERS

St. Patrick's Day, Greetings.

Haply pass the hours,
In gentle sport and mirth,
Mid glowing fields and flowers,
On the day that marks your Birth.

Birthday Greetings

operation with all the dust that was raised. But the compound, a mixture of sand, sawdust and paraffin oil, could be scattered around the floor, let set for a few minutes to hold the dust down, then swept, leaving the floor looking a lot better.

He sold the compound in one hundred-pound kegs for $3.50. He was a good salesman, and I was fascinated with his success. He agreed to sell me a carload of the compound at a discount and give me an exclusive on the territory I was working. However, Rollie and Bill did not like the idea of mixing sweeping compound with illustrated post cards. I had saved a little money myself, and I trudged off to the bank, hoping to get some advice since I certainly didn't expect the owner to loan a teen-age boy any money. But after a short discussion he loaned me the few hundred dollars I needed to complete the payment for the compound. The bank supplied a rubber stamp to endorse checks, which I still have. It reads: Norfolk Brokerage Company — J. C. Hall, Manager.

I thought then that I might combine my sweeping compound business with my "popcorn empire." Now, of course, I realize what a serious mistake these ventures would have been. Popcorn machines were only successful while they were a novelty. And sweeping compound only took an empty shed and a few dollars worth of sand, sawdust and paraffin oil — and anyone could get in the business. In fact, soon there were so many people making the compound that unit sales were very small. Then when streets were paved and floors were covered with linoleum, sweeping compound pretty well dropped out of existence. I learned then never to jump too quickly to conclusions about new products.

In August of 1909 I made my last trip with Rollie to sell post cards and sweeping compound while he sold candy. We stopped in Omaha, and somehow Rollie managed to locate our father. It was the first time we had seen him in over ten years, and it was also the last time we would ever see him. Mother had divorced him by then, and sometime later he moved to California. I explained our business to my father, and he said that Norfolk was too small for wholesaling and that we should move to Omaha. I had already felt the same way, and my father added to my confidence.

That December, Jim Conway, a cigar salesman from Kansas City, visited our store. He was especially fascinating to me because he had been a major league baseball umpire. I told him my plan to move to

Corner of Eleventh and Grand during William Jennings Bryan's 1896 Kansas City visit

Omaha after the first of the year and start a post card business there. He liked the idea but thought I had picked the wrong town.

Conway went to great lengths explaining what he called "the Kansas City spirit." He said the city had gotten the railroad built across the Missouri River at Kansas City, instead of Leavenworth or St. Joseph, where it had been planned. He also told me that the Democratic Convention had been booked in Kansas City for 1900, but three months before the event a fire destroyed the convention hall. Eugene Rust, head of the Swift Packing Company in Kansas City, got the wealthy men in town out of bed the night of the fire to get commitments for enough money to build a new convention hall. Then Rust persuaded the steel mills in Pennsylvania to turn out rush orders. The Democratic National Committee was assured the hall would be ready in time — and it was, the day before the convention opened.

Needless to say, I was impressed by "the Kansas City spirit." It's also possible that I was influenced by the fact that Marie Tracy, the prettiest girl in my class, had moved with her family to Kansas City about six months before. Kansas City, of course, was much larger than Omaha and more centrally located in the country — in fact, almost dead center. It was also a great wholesaling and distributing center with a remarkable network of railroads.

It took some doing to convince my family of the wisdom of a move like this when we had a good little business already going in Norfolk. My strongest selling point was promising that I would go on to school in Kansas City. Finally, I got their reluctant approval. And on January 9, 1910, I boarded a train in Norfolk with a one-way ticket to Kansas City.

PART II:
BUILDING A BUSINESS

The Kansas City Spirit

It was a mighty cold January day when I arrived at the old Union Station in Kansas City at the age of eighteen. At first sight, the city of about 250,000 people seemed mighty cold, too, and I felt very much alone. Since I had two heavy bags, I asked the price of a horse-drawn cab, but it was too much. I trudged up the long wooden chute to the streetcar line. That got me to elevated tracks over the railroad, then through another wooden chute and up a huge bluff to the downtown business district. Things began to look better. And later I learned that the broken-down station where I arrived was being replaced by one of the finest terminals in the country. My confidence in the Kansas City spirit was renewed.

The Baltimore Hotel was said to be the best in town; so I walked over just to see it. It was as grand a hotel as I can remember, built just before the turn of the century with Carrara marble columns and a great fountain. An underground passage led from the bar to the lobby of the Willis Wood Theater. The head hotel chef was a Frenchman, Adrian Delvaux, and as long as he was there the Baltimore was one of the best places I have ever eaten in my life. In 1938 its doors were closed for good.

The hotel, of course, was far too expensive for me, and I set out to find the YMCA. I got a corner room on the top floor, had breakfast and went out to look over the town. My first stop was at Browning, King & Co., where I bought a much-needed overcoat. I got a pair of shoes at a French Shriner and Urner store. I continued to buy shoes from the same man for fifteen years. I walked until lunchtime, when I came across the first cafeteria I had seen. I studied the operation to figure out how it worked.

After lunch I found a barbershop on the lower level of the Altman Building. It was bigger than any barbershop I know of today. The man who cut my hair was one of the proprietors, Earl T. Hedrick — everyone called him Hedrick. When I told him I'd just arrived in Kansas City, he backed away, pointed his scissors at me and said, "Young man, I'm going to give you such a good haircut that when you need another one, you'll come back to me." And I did — for almost fifty years. I followed Hedrick to half a dozen different shops until he retired.

The next morning I registered at Spalding's Commercial College, fulfilling my promise to my family. It was agreed that I would take commercial law, penmanship and spelling. But what I really wanted to learn was how to operate a typewriter. I knew I'd have to type invoices and business letters, because I certainly couldn't afford to have anyone do them for me. George Spalding, the founder's son, was running the school, and he argued that typing wouldn't do me any good unless I also took shorthand. I said I wasn't interested in shorthand since I wasn't going to be taking dictation, I was going to be giving it. He thought I was a little brash but said if I had that much confidence he'd go along with me.

The founder of the school, George E. Spalding, wore a cowboy hat and had white hair with long curls like Buffalo Bill. One afternoon he set up a ladder on a landing between the first and second floors. He called all the students together where they could see him, then climbed the ladder and tacked up a tin sign that read: "Time is money — save time."

That simple slogan made a great impression on me. As my own business grew, I adopted it and changed it to read: "Time is everything — save time." I had already seen that the difference between failure and success was making the best use of time. I never could sit around waiting for things to happen; it's more fun making them happen.

For some time I had been thinking about a mail-order plan for post cards. I picked up maps of Missouri, Kansas and four nearby states. Then I made a record of every town over one thousand population and under ten thousand. My idea was to mail one hundred cards each month to every dealer in these towns. The cards came in packages of one hundred — all of them the same design. I separated the designs and sorted them into new packs of one hundred. Having no office, I stored my inventory under my bed at the YMCA, which was about the only space left in my twelve-by-twelve-foot room.

A little print shop called The Crafters printed our invoices using Kansas City as the home address and Norfolk as a branch office. But the printer thought that a wholesale company (even one located under a bed in the YMCA) should also have a New York office; so one of the women who ran the shop added her brother's Broadway address to the invoices.

Each package of a hundred cards was addressed to "The Leading Post Card Dealer" with the name of the town and state. The enclosed invoice listed "100 Assorted Post Cards" for one dollar plus eight cents for postage. There was often only one dealer in the smallest towns; so the postmaster put the cards in his box. Some, however, wrote and asked for postage to return the undelivered cards or to send a more complete address. A few dealers kept the cards without paying. Some returned them with angry advice. However, about a third sent a check. They would get another shipment the next month, and I gradually built up quite a list. The system worked because few salesmen covered these small towns. Within two months I had two hundred dollars saved and opened a checking account at the First National Bank.

One evening while I was in my room with the door open sorting post cards, a young man walked in and introduced himself. His name was Charles A. Russell, but he said, "Call me Shorty." He asked what I was doing. After I explained, he said he'd like to have a hand in it himself. The idea of selling post cards fascinated him. He started on a commission basis, going out on the road for a week or two at a time. He'd help with any job, even though it was not included in his commission. Shorty was one of the friendliest and most generous people I have ever known.

It wasn't long before the YMCA began to object to my running a mail-order business from my room. And the post office was getting provoked trying to handle all the packages of returned cards in one mailbox. In fact, I had to carry them back to the Y in a suitcase. When school closed for the summer, I rented a small room in the Braley Building for an office and storage space.

A boy named Kim Barnes, who worked for my brothers in Norfolk, wanted to move to Kansas City, and I arranged for him to come. Kim's only goal in life was to become an actor — any kind of an actor. He

Old Union Depot, 1910

Ninth Street Incline, street railway from Depot area to main business district

40

Intersection of Ninth and Main called "The Junction."
Spalding's Commercial College is at left of photograph.

Portrait of Joyce Hall made shortly after his arrival in Kansas City

42

Diner in downtown Kansas City around 1910

Barbershop typical of era

attended some show every night, then he'd go backstage to ask for a job. He would run off with any show that would hire him — and always returned to work for us again. His constant clowning, dancing and singing irritated a hot-headed southern boy who worked for us, Tom Rabey. One morning Tom was opening a case of cards with a small hatchet, and Kim began singing a rousing rendition of "We Will Hang Jeff Davis to a Sour Apple Tree." Tom reared up and threw the hatchet, barely missing Kim's head.

Kim had other eccentricities. He would always top off his breakfast with a piece of pie. I was eating with him one memorable morning when he bit into a sixpenny nail in his apple pie and stuck himself in the roof of his mouth. That discouraged him from eating and singing for a while. Finally, Kim left with a show for good. Some time later I learned he was running a gas station in California.

I began to spend three or four days a week selling out of town. On one trip I was working towns on the Hannibal and St. Joseph Railroad. I had been to Troy, Kansas, and was going on to Hiawatha, but the train was late. I started walking up the tracks to pass the time when I saw the outline of a man in a long dark coat and a black hat coming toward me. It couldn't have been anybody else except the man I had seen at a Chautauqua when I was a small boy — William Jennings Bryan.

I was frightened at the prospect of running into him, but he reached me before I could get away. We talked for a good part of the afternoon. When the train finally arrived, Bryan and I boarded together and went on to Hiawatha. As we were pulling into the station, we saw piles of peaches by the side of the tracks. Evidently the price had gone so low for peaches that a grower couldn't afford the shipping costs and just dumped them. Bryan picked up two or three and began eating with great relish. So did I.

We set off for the hotel, which cost two dollars a day and included meals. Bryan asked me to have supper with him. I was scared all the time but tried to remember that he was the Great Commoner. Bryan had a substantial appetite, and after a big meal, the dessert came — canned peaches. Bryan called the owner and told him: "Here you go out and buy canned peaches when right down by the station there are fresh peaches by the bucketful." The owner rushed off to the station and returned with fresh peaches for our dessert. Bryan was probably the most important person who had ever set foot in that town.

44

It may seem a strange statement, but by fall I couldn't afford to go back to school. If I hadn't spent all my time running the business, I probably would have lost it altogether. It was no longer just a sideline. In fact, we had already outgrown our quarters and rented an adjoining room in the same building.

The Crafters Print Shop was on the second floor, with one small press and a hand cutter. They were good typesetters. Their work was usually run on a light brown stock with dark brown ink in keeping with the popular trend. I decided to print some of our own post cards with quotations by famous men. This was my first publishing experience. I began to think more about the importance of quality and how it could be controlled by publishing and manufacturing our own products.

By now I was convinced that illustrated post cards were really a passing fancy — a dated custom that would have to be replaced by something else. Post cards were not really a means of communication between people. Most of them were either humorous or simply decorative and sent because it was the thing to do.

Personal communication was practically limited to writing letters. But as the pace of life was picking up, people had less time to write long thoughtful letters. Telephones were relatively new, and calling long distance was almost unheard of. On top of that, there were two telephone systems in Kansas City, the Bell Company and the Home Company. About half the people were on one system and half on the other, and you could only talk to people on the same system. I still can't think of anything you need two of less than you need two telephone systems.

Kansas City itself was an inspiration to me that first year. It was a lively town, less than half a century away from the old Santa Fe Trail days. While I had little time for recreation, I did play baseball on Sundays with the YMCA team, usually as a pinch hitter. After I struck out one too many times, I gave that up. I was much better at basketball. At six feet, I was tall for those days and played with a team called the Tigers in the city league. Even then I spent most of my time on the bench in cold Armory Hall. I finally had my moment of glory after a game ended in a tie and remained tied after a five-minute playoff. Only then did the coach send me in, and I had a hard time deciding whether to play or give him a kick in the shins. Just before the bell rang to end the second playoff, I made a one-handed

45

shot over my head — and astonished the crowd, not to mention myself. By luck the ball fell through to break the tie. On that note I ended my basketball career. However, the memorable thing about it was not that game, but a fellow I met playing it — Charles S. Stevenson, who was to become a very important part of building Hallmark Cards.

About the only other recreation I found time for was the theater. Kansas City was then the best theater town between Chicago and San Francisco. There were three legitimate theaters, the Willis Wood, the Schubert and the Grand, with road productions of Broadway shows. I attended at least once a week with Jim Jackson, the drama critic of the *Kansas City Star*, who had two good tickets to each show in town. When Jim wasn't available, Shorty Russell, Kim Barnes and I would get tickets in the second gallery for twenty-five cents apiece.

We saw some of the best theater of the time, with performers like The Barrymores, Al Jolson, Sarah Bernhardt, Southern and Marlow, Lillian Russell, Richard Mansfield, Jeanne Eagels, William Gillette, Eddie Cantor, Fred Stone, George M. Cohan, the Marx Brothers, Fritzi Scheff and David Warfield.

I developed a keen interest and appreciation for good theater, so much so that even in those early, lean years I made occasional trips to New York to see Broadway shows. The first one was as memorable as any that followed — *Madame X* with Laurette Taylor in 1910. However, Broadway itself was a great disappointment. I expected it to be paved in gold; instead, it was crowded and dirty with a lot of cheap little stores.

All the same, I always found New York exciting. And on my first trip, like everybody else, I went to Grant's Tomb and visited the Flat Iron Building, which was the big attraction. The Empire State Building didn't exist until 1931. Some of the importers of cards we bought took me to Luchow's for lunch and Delmonico's for dinner. The most exotic thing to me was being served raw oysters, opened fresh in front of my eyes.

This was also the start of motion picture era. Nickelodeons arrived in downtown Kansas City for five cents admission. Heim's Electric Park opened in the summer. Its main attractions were a fountain with beautiful lights playing on it and a pavilion with a band concert every night; even John Philip Sousa appeared. While it was called an amusement park, with pleasure rides and game stands, I think of it more as a miniature Disneyland.

In fact, Walt Disney lived in Kansas City at the time, and it's possible that Electric Park was in the back of his mind when he started dreaming of Disneyland. (In later years I suggested this to him, but he would never admit it.) He attended Benton Grade School, and one of his classmates was a very pretty girl named Elizabeth Dilday. Disney delivered the *Kansas City Star* to her parents' home. She remembered him as the boy who was always drawing. I know, because I later met and married Elizabeth. Some years later, Walt's creations were used on our greeting cards, and we became good friends.

Kansas City has always had one of the finest park and boulevard systems in the country, largely because of the enthusiasm and ability of an engineer named August R. Meyer. And in 1896 Colonel Thomas H. Swope gave the city almost fourteen hundred acres to establish a park — the second largest in the country. On Sundays people slicked up their horses, washed their buggies and went out for a drive on the great boulevards. The sidewalks were lined with people watching the elegant carriages with uniformed coachmen.

One of the most important and aggressive community leaders was William Rockhill Nelson, who later left most of his estate to build the Nelson Gallery of Art, one of the nation's finest museums. His *Kansas City Star* was an outstanding newspaper. Two of its writers were Ernest Hemingway, who started as a cub reporter in 1917, and William Allen White, who wrote editorials. Pulitzer Prize winner Henry J. Haskell was the chief editorial writer. Roy Roberts became the *Star's* legendary managing editor in 1928 and later its president.

J. C. Nichols did more to improve the environment in Kansas City than any man I know of in any other town in the United States. In 1905 he started to build a residential district that is still a model for the entire country. And in 1922 he developed an adjoining shopping area known as the Country Club Plaza, the first such shopping center in the country and still one experts come to study.

Kansas City had outstanding merchants, too, such as the T. M. James family (yes, descendants of Jesse James), who were china wholesalers and retailers. Fred Wolferman stores were just becoming famous when I arrived. He was considered one of the greatest merchants of all time because he knew how to "glorify a cabbage." And Kansas City was the headquarters for Fred Harvey, "the father of good eating for the traveling public." He was copied universally, but never equaled.

Willis Wood Theater

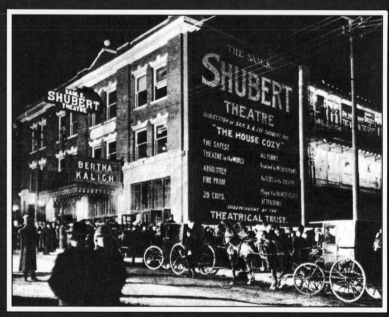

Shubert Theater

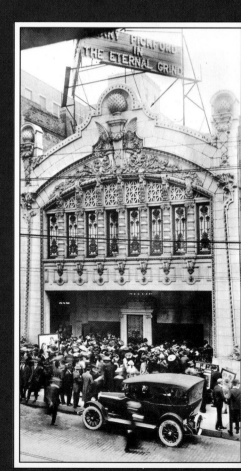

Royal Theater

48

Post card depicting Heim's Electric Park

Heim's Electric Park

Wolferman's, a fine Kansas City grocery store

Petticoat Lane, the windiest street in downtown Kansas City

Petticoat Lane, looking West from Grand Avenue, Kansas City.

View of The Paseo, a part of Kansas City's highly acclaimed park and boulevard system

House in the Country Club district, J.C. Nichols development

William Rockhill Nelson, civic leader and founder of the Kansas City Star

Home of the Kansas City Star

Shelter House at Swope Park, 1912

Zoo at Swope Park

The city had a minor-league baseball team then, but the Blues in the old American Association drew major-league-size crowds. Meat packing was the top industry, and Kansas City was the second largest wholesale drug center. It was also the second largest railroad terminal and ranked first in the number of lines entering and leaving.

The Kansas City spirit had become part of my life. This was the city where I would settle, and I was convinced my family should, too. Our business was growing, and I believed in its future. When the new year rolled around, 1911, my mother, Rollie and Marie joined me in Kansas City. We bought a comfortable house on Troost Avenue at Manheim Road. It had been a long year alone.

Union Station, Kansas City, Mo.

Post card published by Hall Brothers

When You Get to the End of Your Rope

Rollie had to give up a good position selling in Nebraska to take a chance with me on an idea that must have sounded risky. But Rollie believed in me as much as I believed in him — and I felt sure we could make a modest success of the business together. For the first few years in Kansas City, Rollie and I didn't even draw salaries. We only spent money when it was absolutely necessary.

Rollie made a great contribution in those early years as the core of our selling organization. He set a permanent standard for our sales philosophy — he never used pressure, he sold his product because he believed in it and he never sold anything that he didn't think a dealer could sell himself. His customers were his friends, and I can't recall Rollie ever losing a customer — or a friend. As a salesman, he was not particularly imaginative or aggressive, but he was industrious and every ounce a gentleman.

The two of us could have continued selling our cards ourselves, but I couldn't see that ever becoming a big business. I felt we had to have salesmen even if they cost more money than we could make in the beginning. Rollie was against it, and considering our finances, any sensible man probably would have agreed with him. "We haven't even got the money for their expenses," Rollie argued. But with some long-term credit, we went ahead, hiring men on a commission basis.

I was only twenty years old and looked even younger. It wasn't easy hiring men who were sometimes twice my age — or even more. A veteran salesman would take one look at me and shake his head. How could a boy run a business? Sometimes even dealers would brush me off. One I invited to visit our operation in Kansas City simply asked, "Is this all you got?" And he walked out saying, "What the hell did you have me come up here for?" Sometimes I wonder if I would have succeeded if things had come easily. As it was, I had to do a little bit of everything myself, which is a good way to really learn the business.

Rollie went out on two- and three-week trips, covering the most productive business towns. I worked the areas closest to Kansas City so I could easily get back and forth. Finally, I decided that instead of traveling by train, an automobile would be more convenient and even cheaper. I bought a Hupmobile, then the most up-to-date of the low-priced cars. It was a four-door touring car, which was advertised as having "a one-man folding top." It would have been more accurate if the ad had said "a four-man folding top." A Prestolite tank on the running board furnished gas for the headlights. The tank was simply strapped on, and after having it stolen a few times, I was careful where I parked after dark. It cost eighteen dollars to replace. The taillight, in a small metal container with a wick, burned coal oil.

Few roads were paved, and in northern Missouri the soil was mostly gumbo. Now you may think of gumbo as something to eat, but it is the waxiest, stickiest mud there is after a good rain. Several times I was mired in a mudhole overnight until I could get a farmer with a team of horses to pull me out the next day. On one trip to St. Louis, I had to change tires eleven times. You had to clamp a metal cup, which held about an ounce of gasoline, over a rubber patch; then light the patch to vulcanize it to the tube. The tube was then inflated with a hand pump. Automobiling wasn't all that fun then. I just thought it was.

By the fall of 1911, we had become so crowded we rented the third floor of a building at 915 Broadway. I thought this space — 20' x 115' — would take care of us for many years. It was the first time we had room for two desks, a flat-top and a secondhand cherry rolltop. We worked six days a week from seven in the morning until six at night.

By 1912, we found that post cards were not selling as well as the previous year. To increase our business, we had to add new territories. Manufacturers had made the mistake of cheapening the quality of cards, and dime stores started selling them for ten cents a dozen. The public was having less and less to do with them.

It wasn't hard to see that greeting cards would have more of a future than post cards. We added valentines to our line, which had the effect of bridging the gap between illustrated post cards and greeting cards. Many of them were sent in envelopes, whereas post cards were handicapped because there was no secrecy to the messages. I began to see that greeting cards were more than a form of communication — they were a social custom. While the carriage trade had never taken post cards very seriously, they would buy greeting cards of the finest quality.

For many years, they were not even called greeting cards but simply Easter cards or Christmas cards. And most of them were imported from England and Germany. Late in the nineteenth century, Louis Prang of Boston published beautifully lithographed cards that could be called greeting cards. Prang introduced his own multicolor printing, using as many as twenty colors on a card. His cards were equally impressive for their paper, design and lettering. And he used the most talented artists of the day. Many of his cards had silk fringe around the edges, and a few sold for as much as three dollars.

Prang published Christmas, Easter, Valentine's Day, birthday and New Year's cards. (It was the custom on New Year's Day to leave cards at the homes of friends.) His cards were superior to the best ones being imported from England, and he set a standard of quality for the entire industry. Eventually, Prang sold about five million cards a year.

Early in the twentieth century, several firms started selling greeting cards with envelopes. The George C. Whitney Company of Massachusetts was the largest manufacturer of valentines. They produced millions of little penny valentines for school children and also large handmade valentines with elaborate scrolls and folded Celluloid that sold from fifty cents up to ten dollars.

We added a line of leather post cards by stamping a hot plate on real leather to burn in the design. They retailed for ten cents and had what we called "wisecracks" printed on them. A popular one was: "The Cowboy's Creed — Live every day so you can look any man in the eye and tell him to go straight to hell." Some of our customers objected to it, but it struck me as good advice. Another that impressed me even more, because it was so close to the truth for us, was: "When you get to the end of your rope, tie a knot in it and hang on."

Many times in the years of building our business, I found that was about all I could do. The novelty post cards kept us alive for a time. While they were produced with quality, they did not appeal to the carriage trade. The largest-selling post card over a long period of time had a simple message in bold type: "SMILE, damn you, smile." This was advice I had difficulty taking myself. There were not many light moments during

Post card sent by Rollie, (Right), to his mother

POST CARD

SEATTLE. WASH.
JUL 8
11:30 PM
1909

WORLD
FAIR
SEATTLE
1909

CORRESPONDENCE HERE

NAME AND ADDRESS HERE

Dear Mama
I bought an
automobile.
Rollie.

Mrs. N. D. Ha
Norfol
℅ Hill's Book Store

56

Joyce Hall in his first car

Jim Short, the first salesman

First Hall Brothers employees

Harry Lange, New York salesman

MIDST THOU BUT KNOW HOW FERVENTLY I LOVE THEE.

All happiness be thine this Christmastide.

THE LIGHT OF OUR HOME

Going to My Valentine.

A Merry Christmas.

Nineteenth Century greeting cards representing the work of Prang, Volland, Whitney and others

From all harm may Love protect thee,
And the star of Faith direct thee!

BEAUTY AND JOY AND ALL GOOD CHEER! YOUNG CHRISTMAS COMES BUT ONCE A YEAR.

those early years — and I suffered all my life from just barely smiling when I should have grinned and grinning when I should have laughed.

We had learned a lot about selling at the retail level from our experience at the Norfolk store. And this we shared with our dealers. We'd recommend certain cards with confidence and steer them away from others. Rollie's direct, honest approach always worked to his advantage, and I followed his example. A dealer would say, "I'll take one hundred of these." I'd tell him, "I'll be glad to sell them to you, but first let me show you some cards that might sell even better." I also learned that it was better to take poor-selling cards out of the line altogether. My records on sales of individual cards were all in my head. The only thing I put on paper was what people owed us.

This was my first experience with product research, and it laid the groundwork for the records we have kept over the years on the retail performance of our products. We were soon to apply these lessons to our first retail business, which we had been thinking of getting into all the time.

Toward the end of 1913, we found a store in a good location with half of the first floor for lease. It also had a full basement where we could handle our stock and fill orders. It was ideal for our purposes, and we could have it ready for the Christmas trade. In the meantime, a phonograph and record firm in Chicago came to town looking for space. They wanted to take over the entire store. The landlord agreed; then I tried to lease all the space, but was told that the Chicago firm was a better financial risk. But they went broke, and we are still paying our bills.

Another store of similar size was available across the street in the Corn Belt Bank Building. By this time, it was too late to be of any use for the Christmas selling season. We moved early in 1914 and put together a good showing of cards and stationery. We soon added the products of Raphael Tuck & Sons of London, probably the oldest and largest manufacturer of cards, calendars and children's books.

About this time, I started to transfer my mental records on the sale of cards to paper. Then, late one night, I got the idea of rating the cards based on their sales. We were able to tell our dealers which cards would sell and which wouldn't and to take them out of the line if they didn't. Then we'd replace them with another line of our cards. Our competitors simply didn't have this information. The system not only improved our sales, it also improved our products. Our methods were considered revolutionary at a time when the idea was to sell anything any way you could.

The P. F. Volland Company in Chicago was the most quality-minded competitor we had. Paul Volland was a very creative man. His enthusiasm and desire for quality were an education to me. But he wasn't always practical, which had me watching for pitfalls to avoid. Still, Volland always profited by his mistakes and consistently built a bigger and better business.

Some years after I met him, Volland was contacted by an elderly woman who had a ceramic medallion with a likeness of George Washington molded into it. He decided to reproduce it. The woman hoped to make a great deal of money on royalties. However, Volland ran into difficulties reproducing it, and it was not a success. She became suspicious that she wasn't being treated fairly and confronted Volland in his office. Before he could fully explain the problem, she opened her handbag, pulled out a small revolver and killed him. He had been my closest friend in the industry, and I have often thought of the further contributions he could have made had he lived.

By now, we were certain that post cards had had their day — and a long one at that. Having introduced engraved cards with envelopes, such as for Christmas, we were ready to bet our future on them. I went to Chicago to make a deal with the Murray Engraving Company to wholesale their line exclusively in our territory. The Murray cards sold well to the better trade and gave our line considerable prestige.

Without notice, a salesman from Murray called on us — not to show me the new line and take our order as I expected. He wanted our order, but only as retailers, not wholesalers. Murray had decided to put a man in our territory to sell his line directly. I went to Chicago to see him, but his decision was final. Once again, it looked as if we were in trouble. We had to have engraved cards — and soon.

A small concern in Kansas City, the Smith-Pierce Engraving Company, had done excellent work for a number of years. I asked if they could engrave some designs for us — a poinsettia, a holly wreath, a vase with roses and two others. We used different sentiments on each of the designs, giving us a line of twenty cards of varied sizes and colors. They sold out in all the stores, but the small runs kept them from being profitable. It was the first use of our name on any merchandise — "Published by Hall Bros., Kansas City, Mo., Made in U.S.A."

Now we were publishers.

Nineteen fifteen began as one of those years when we were truly at the end of our rope. We had just received our valentine shipments, unpacked them and were ready to fill orders. About five o'clock on the morning of January 11, 1915, I had a telephone call from Reed Gentry, an officer in the small bank that occupied half of our building. He was an easygoing fellow and said: "Hall, your place is on fire." "I'll be right down," I said. "Don't hurry," he said. "It's all burned down."

I slipped a pair of pants over my pajamas, put on some shoes and an overcoat and rushed down to the store. He was right. Everything that was burnable had burned except a few things in the basement that were under several feet of water.

The small iron safe that contained all our records — accounts, orders and the little cash we had — was partially underwater. It was an old safe we had acquired inexpensively, and I had no idea whether or not it was waterproof. If our records had been destroyed, we wouldn't have been able to bill anyone. We would have been bankrupt. I ran a block up the street to a draying firm. A wagon was standing there hitched to two big horses. They pulled the safe out. Although the water had been pouring over it for some time, the dial on the safe was still so hot it burned my fingers. But it opened and was dry inside.

Nevertheless, our entire supply of valentines, for which we were heavily in debt, had been destroyed. I was almost in a state of shock. But there's a big difference between being shocked and being whipped. If we had wanted to quit, this would have been a good time to do it. It was near-zero weather, and I stood there shivering with our small staff, watching the smoldering fire. I looked at the debris in the basement, wondering what to do about several thousand dollars in valentine orders and no valentines to send.

At this point, a well-dressed young man introduced himself as Willard Rupe, the manager of the Starr Piano Company, which was located a few doors from us on the second floor of the old *Kansas City Star* Building. He said he had leased part of his space for future use; then added some of the nicest words I've ever heard: "You're welcome to use the space without any charge." He even furnished a typewriter, some tables and chairs. This was probably the most generous thing anybody had ever done for me. We stayed there several years and paid rent every month in spite of Rupe's reluctance to take it.

By ten o'clock the same morning, we were operating again. I called our two principal suppliers of valentines, explained what had happened and asked if they could duplicate their shipments as soon as possible. One of them, Simon Bergman, said he could, but asked how we were going to pay for them. I said I didn't know when we could pay, but assured him we would. He got part of the shipment out by express the same day. When I told the other supplier what Bergman had done, he agreed to do the same.

Since there was no inventory, it wasn't hard to figure out our financial worth. Even with the nine thousand dollars insurance, I estimated we were seventeen thousand dollars in the red. Someone said, "Hall, you're starting all over again from scratch." "That isn't so," I told him. "We aren't starting from scratch. We're starting from seventeen thousand dollars behind scratch."

While the salesmen were waiting for samples to be assembled after the fire, one of them, Jack Burroughs, would disappear down the back stairs to a bar across the alley. He was a good salesman but didn't always tend to his knitting. He would get to feeling good and start writing poetry. Finally, I told him that if he was going to use his time that way, he should try to write some card sentiments. They didn't amount to much at first. Then one day he sketched a puppy on the corner of a card with these words:

> *Not little like this tiny pup,*
> *But big, just like a dog grown up.*
> *I'm wishing you a Merry Christmas.*

I thought it might sell and asked him to do more. After several tries, he came to me with one that read:

> *I sit, by heck, and scratch my neck,*
> *And wonder what I'll send you,*
> *Thoughts wander through my muddled brain,*
> *From buzz wagon to candy cane,*
> *But none of these quite suits this year,*
> *So I'll just send a word of cheer.*

63

I said, "Jack, I don't think you've finished it; just add 'A Merry Christmas.' "

While they may not seem very clever today, these were the first humorous sentiments used on greeting cards for special occasions. And they were an immediate success. Our business was still small, and it gave me a lot of satisfaction that the larger publishers began imitating the style of these new cards.

In March of 1915, we hired Evert Wampler, who was to work for us for over fifty years. He didn't tell us his age, only that he had a permit from the state employment office. As it turned out, he was only twelve, though much older in appearance. To get the permit, he had fudged two years on his age. He had to work since he was the sole support of his mother. This was something I could understand.

Being just a boy, he was quite rambunctious. On one occasion, I heard a lot of commotion in the next room and opened the door. Evert was armed with an oil-soaked rag and was about to throw it at someone. He saw me, hesitated just a second, then threw it anyway. I had warned Evert I'd fire him the next time I caught him horsing around. But I didn't. I think I might have if he *hadn't* thrown it. It seemed to me that anyone with that kind of gumption in front of the boss must be a pretty good man — and he proved to be that and more.

He began as a pressman's helper on the first cards completely produced in our plant. He was intelligent and industrious and eventually became the director of our extensive mechanical research operation.

When Evert retired at the age of sixty-five in 1967, our board of directors passed a "Resolution of Appreciation" stating that he would "forever be known as the only Hallmark employee to complete more than a half century of service." Evert remains a consultant to Hallmark to this day, and he's just as likeable and effective as he ever was.

It was still 1915 when I learned the Smith-Pierce Engraving Company was in financial trouble. They had bought their presses on time and couldn't keep up the payments. We arranged to have the presses turned over to us by assuming their debt, and Gus Smith and Herbert Pierce both came to work for us. We began experimenting with our own cards. Gus Smith engraved some new dies for Christmas designs, and we hired several women to add hand coloring to the engravings.

We were manufacturers.

By the time we got into our heavy selling season in 1915, we had a more interesting line than ever before. And we had another advantage over our competitors — we were not handicapped by any old merchandise. The fire had taken care of that. But the most important thing was that we were producing a good many of our own cards, on our own presses, in our own plant.

So the year that had started with disaster ended on the highest note to date.

Leather card

Moving Experiences

One thing we had resisted almost at the risk of losing our business was going into debt. Evidently we looked like a fairly good risk to some bankers, and a man from the Corn Belt Bank came to call on me. He and the president looked over our operation and offered to loan us three thousand dollars. This came as quite a surprise since I didn't think anyone would go out of his way to loan money to a struggling business like ours. I accepted only after making a strong point that I couldn't pay off the loan until Christmas, when most of our money came in.

However, about midsummer as I was passing the bank, the president rapped on the window and motioned me in. His discount board (I think he called it) was getting restless and wanted a payment on the loan. I reminded him of our agreement, but he said, "Well, times are tighter now." He continued to rap on the window at me every now and then when I'd pass.

Then still another bank, Traders National, said they had been impressed by our working evenings and weekends and were interested in our account. That was fine, I told them, if they'd loan me three thousand dollars until after Christmas. The president, J. R. Dominick, asked me why I needed the money, and when I told him, he smiled and agreed.

It was a great moment when I paid off the Corn Belt Bank and withdrew my account. The president tried to convince me I was making a mistake, but I said my experience to date had indicated otherwise. From then on I was not hesitant about passing his window.

During the years of establishing our business, it seems I was to meet at least one representative from every investigatory division of the federal government. In 1917 a man came to talk to me about income taxes. He wanted to know why we hadn't made out a return, since the income tax law was made effective in 1913. I told him that we hadn't made any money since 1913 to report. In fact, we hadn't made any money since we started the business in 1910, but this would be our first moderately profitable year, even though we'd still be heavily in debt.

In no uncertain terms he informed me that it made no difference whether or not we showed any profit; we still had to submit annual returns. Further, we would have to *prove* that we had made no profit since 1913. We would have to prepare a record of our inventory at the beginning of the year and the close. And it would have to be supported with evidence of our financial transactions. I said I simply wasn't capable of doing such a job, and he recommended an accountant. Everybody was put to work taking inventory. The accountant worked on the books for weeks and finally produced tax returns. Since we only showed losses, we were not penalized.

The United States entered the war on April 6, 1917, and industry generally was in a state of confusion. So were we. There was beginning to be a demand for cards to send servicemen. We made some that were tied with red, white and blue ribbons and featured military symbols. But we soon found out that the men really wanted cards just like those sent at home.

On one card we made for servicemen, we rolled cellophane around a cigarette, twisted the ends, then glued it to the card with an appropriate sentiment. It was extremely popular. We had produced thousands of them when a gentleman walked into our office with several in hand. He identified himself as a federal revenue inspector. He said that each card was a special transaction that required an individual cigarette tax stamp, and it didn't matter that the stamp had been paid on each package. With a little mental arithmetic I realized this would run into a staggering amount of money. The inspector said he realized we had been acting in good faith, even if uninformed. He agreed that if we destroyed the remaining stock and made no more, he wouldn't proceed any further with the matter.

It was during this same period that we had a visit from the U. S. Treasury office. Jack Burroughs had written one of his humorous sentiments that read simply:

Tho it takes my last red cent,
I'll consider it well spent,
To send a bit of merriment to you.

At the top of the card we had an engraving of an exact copy of a one-cent piece. The card had been on the market for about a year when the agent came by.

Didn't I know that it was against federal law to duplicate currency? Because the coin was not metal and was printed on only one side, I didn't see any problem. After giving me a severe lecture, he said if I'd destroy all the penny cards we had on hand, he would consider the matter closed. The card had been such a good seller that I asked him if we could continue making it if we changed the word *cent* on the die of the coin to read "last red cent." He agreed, and we continued to sell the card for many years.

After these experiences, before we did anything unusual, I inquired about its legality. But there was still a lot I was to learn about publishing greeting cards — and the next lesson came fast.

A few years earlier an elderly man had brought us a poem and asked how much it would cost to have it printed on one hundred greeting cards. There were two verses that read:

I'd like to be the sort of friend that you have been to me.
I'd like to be the help that you are always glad to be,
I'd like to mean as much to you each minute of the day
As you have meant, Good Friend of Mine, to me along the way.
And this is just to wish somehow that I could but repay
A portion of the gladness that you've strewn along my way,
For could I have one wish today, this only would it be,
I'd like to be the sort of friend that you have been to me!

It was a natural for greeting cards. I asked the man where he got it, and he said, "I wrote it myself." I told him we'd engrave one hundred quality cards for him free if we could use the sentiment. He was delighted with the arrangement.

We made the cards with the sentiment handsomely engraved next to hand-painted poinsettias. We simply changed the fifth line to read: "I'm wishing at this Christmas time that I could but repay." It proved to be our best-selling Christmas card, and later we adapted the sentiment for other occasions. We tried to get the old man to write more, but he showed no interest, and we lost track of him.

In 1921 I was in the store we had opened in Chicago when an

elegant gentleman wearing a Prince Albert frock coat and swinging a cane asked for the proprietor. He was in a severe stage of agitation, demanding to know where we got the sentiment. He said he was Mr. Reilly of Reilly & Lee Company in Chicago, and the poem was published by him in a book of Edgar A. Guest's entitled *A Heap o' Livin*. The poem, of course, was *A Friend's Greeting*. "You had no right to use it," Reilly explained. I told him again how we had come by it, but he didn't seem to believe me. He marched out of the store and soon returned with a copy of the book. He demanded that we destroy all the cards, as well as the plates, and said he would probably still sue us for damages.

When he finally quieted down, I asked if there wasn't some arrangement we could make to continue publishing the card. He said I couldn't pay him enough money to make it worthwhile. Realizing the importance of the card in our line, finally, in desperation, I told him I would give him five hundred dollars for the exclusive use of the sentiment on greeting cards. I couldn't believe my own offer. The going rate was about one dollar a line; this amounted to over sixty dollars a line. It was probably the most money ever paid at that time for one sentiment.

It had quite a stabilizing effect on him, and he asked, "How are you going to pay for it?" I said by check, but he wanted cash. So before he signed our agreement, we walked up to the bank where he could cash the check. From then on he'd occasionally stop in our store to see if there was anything else we could use from his book lines.

Almost everyone felt that we'd never make our money back on this investment, but the poem was so right for greeting cards that I couldn't give it up. It turned out to be one of the best investments we ever made, and *A Friend's Greeting* — or *My Friend*, as it's often called — continued to be a best seller on cards for many years. Even to this day, it sells well in the Hallmark line. With the success of this card, we made arrangements directly with Edgar Guest to write sentiments for us. I became very fond of Edgar Guest. He was a wonderful gentleman, always accommodating. We remained good friends throughout his life.

Gift-wrapping paper — or as we called it then, "gift dressing" — in those days consisted only of plain white, red and green tissue and one holly pattern. Most packages were tied with tinsel cord, and a few fastidious people used good ribbon from a dry-goods store. Before Christmas in 1917 we had already sold out our entire stock of the paper. Rollie went to our plant to see if there was anything else customers might use to wrap packages. He picked up an armful of fancy, decorated envelope linings imported from France. They were about the size of a sheet of wrapping paper. We stacked them on top of a showcase.

We charged ten cents a sheet, and I never saw anything accepted so quickly. Customers acted as if they were at a half-price sale. The next year we put them up in a package of three sheets for twenty-five cents. We thought we had placed a large enough order but, again, sold out before Christmas. After the war we bought some American-made papers along with the French ones and created cards to go with them.

We didn't realize it then, but for all practical purposes, an entire new industry had been born. In fact, the decorative gift-wrapping business was born the day Rollie placed the French envelope linings on top of our showcase. Soon gift-wrapping paper became the first product we made that was a departure from greeting cards.

One of our major suppliers of cards, Simon Bergman of the Illustrated Postcard and Novelty Company in New York, had always said that when he made $250,000, he was going to retire. I wasn't concerned about losing his services, because I didn't believe anybody could make $250,000 in a lifetime.

However, I didn't think Bergman was altogether fair to me. While he was doing a good business with us, he was also backing one of our direct competitors, the Elite Post Card Company. Elite had gone bankrupt twice, and we purchased their stock on both occasions. Still, Bergman revived Elite and continued to finance them.

Bergman's invoices would arrive with about seven pages covering a great many items. They were written in meticulous longhand by an old German fellow who worked for him. On the invoice for our Christmas orders one year, I noticed that a sizeable amount had been left off the bill — totalling about eighteen hundred dollars. Because Bergman had been so difficult, I wrestled with my conscience about what to do with the eighteen-hundred-dollar bonanza. But I knew I couldn't live with it and wrote to Bergman. It gave me a lot of relief, even though it nearly broke my heart to do it.

Naturally, Bergman was pleased — and even more surprised — that a customer would call his attention to such an advantageous error. From then on we had a much better relationship, and our volume with him increased.

It wasn't much later that I learned Bergman was about to retire. He had made his quarter million and was closing his plant. The loss of his services would cripple us. I called one of Bergman's sales representatives, Harry Driscoll, to ask if it would be possible to buy Bergman's manufacturing equipment. It was Driscoll's understanding that the equipment was to be taken over by one of our competitors. That set me back all over again. But Driscoll said he would talk to Bergman. Bergman called to invite me to meet with him in New York. He made it clear that he was doing so because he remembered my informing him about the discrepancy in his invoice.

Bergman had had an appraisal made on the equipment, then startled me by saying that he thought several pieces were overvalued. He offered them to me at a lower price than the appraisal. It was clear that he could sell the equipment for more than he was charging me. We had only six pieces of manufacturing equipment at the time. With this purchase we would be adding twenty more — a significant expansion for us long before we would normally have been able to afford it. Bergman put no deadline on my note promising to pay for the equipment — just whenever we had the money — and he charged no interest. Since the war was still on, we probably would have had no chance to expand. Even if we could have afforded it, new equipment was not available to buy. And there was no way of predicting how much longer the war would last.

Some months later, on a Monday morning, I was attending a businessmen's breakfast in Wolferman's Tiffin Room. A spellbinding speaker was about halfway through a talk about selling Liberty Bonds, which businessmen were expected to do. The date was November 11, 1918. Sirens began to blow and bells rang. Everybody was out on the streets. The war had ended.

Certainly no one in the greeting card business set out to benefit from the war, but in many ways it was an important turning point for the industry. People sought closer contact with one another and especially with their relatives and friends in the service. And servicemen themselves not only enjoyed receiving greeting cards but sending them as well. As a result many more men became permanent buyers of cards than ever before. And I saw something else in the custom — a way of giving less articulate people, and those who tend to disguise their feelings, a voice to express their love and affection.

We were at 1114 Grand in 1919 when I got my first private office. It was about the size of one of our elevators today and just barely took in my old cherry rolltop desk and a swivel-spring chair. And there was room for a small chair for a visitor.

A mischievous young girl, Bertha Bauer, was working for us. One day when I stepped out of my office, I saw her at the drinking fountain. She had a paper cup of water and was sprinkling everyone around her. I called Bertie into my office and closed the door. I was trying to decide whether to fire her or just give her a stern lecture. She had a winning smile and an engaging manner that made either of these alternatives difficult. But I was determined that some action had to be taken.

I leaned back in my swivel chair, like a big executive, and the spring on the darned thing broke. I went over backwards, and, being quite tall, there wasn't room for both me and the chair on the floor behind my desk. It created such a commotion that other employees rushed in to help. I certainly needed it, because I was so badly tangled in the chair that I couldn't get to my feet. In any case, this young lady reformed her ways and even went to night school to improve her shorthand. She became my secretary and was an excellent one for a good many years.

My small office always proved large enough for an occasional crisis. One of our salesmen, Harry Runyan, was a proper gentleman, always dressed like an ad in a magazine. But he didn't work quite as hard as the other salesmen, and I decided to have a serious talk with him.

It wasn't long before I heard fire engines clanging down the street. They stopped in front of our place. I went to the open window, and water came spraying into my office. The awning just below was blazing. Runyan smoked tailor-made cigarettes and had thrown one out the window, setting the awning on fire. Another disciplinary discussion ended in chaos.

That same summer, Arthur Newell, a florist, asked me to consider a young man, a real go-getter, for a job. His name was Charles S. Stevenson, a top sergeant just out of the army. I remembered that Charlie and I had played basketball together when I first arrived in Kansas City, and he had been the star.

After two or three interviews with Stevenson, I could tell he was a good man. I didn't know where to use him, but I didn't want to pass him up. Charlie reported for work on July 21, 1919. I had him listing orders from dealers to be sure we had enough stock on hand. This was a monotonous job and certainly not good enough for a bright and ambitious top sergeant. Charlie would quit almost every Saturday afternoon. He'd tell me this was no place for him — he wasn't going to sit around listing orders for a living. I'd talk him into staying for another week, but he'd be right back the next Saturday.

Finally, I asked him, "What do you want to do?" Well, he had been to our basement storage room under the Mercer Jewelry Company where we kept our out-of-season stock. He wanted to take Bob Edwards, our porter, and Julian Raines, a stock boy who stuttered badly, over there with him to straighten the place out. I was relieved that Charlie had invented a job for himself.

In the meantime, we were having problems with rats in our main place. The building was mill-constructed and right across the alley from a large restaurant. Someone told me that the way to get rid of rats was to bring in a couple of ferrets. They're like weasels — and bigger and stronger than rats. We got two of them.

We kept them in a cage during the day and released them at night to hunt rats. This method of abolishing rats had some disadvantages. In a place with as many high bins, stacked shipping cases and packing materials, it was often a bigger job rounding up the ferrets than ferreting out the rats. And the ferrets scared the girls a lot more than they did the rats. A number of mornings got off to a bad start when we'd be chasing the ferrets — and the girls would be running in all directions.

It came to an end after a ferret had chased a rat — or vice versa — into an empty metal drum. We were never quite sure who was the pursuer and who was the pursuee. In any case, being unable to get out of the drum, the ferret and the rat struck up an amiable truce and gave each other no further trouble.

Finally, we moved the ferrets to the storage basement, where Charlie and his two-man crew were putting things in order — and where there were no girls working. Charlie and Bob were moving cases in the front when Julian came running out from the dark in the back. He stuttered badly when things were normal — now he couldn't even be understood. He was jiggling and jumping and pointing when finally Bob caught on that a ferret had chased a rat right up the inside of his pants leg. The rat made a sizeable lump, and Julian grabbed it by both ends and wrapped it in the loose part of his pants. Bob took the handle of a broom and cracked the rat over the head — without doing much damage to Julian's leg.

Someone told me about professional rat exterminators, and I hired one. By the time we got around to building our own plants, we made sure they were rat proof.

For the most part, our stock records were still kept in my head. When Charlie Stevenson found a hundred or so packing cases with no labels on them, he'd ask me what they contained. I simply knew by the size and appearance of the cases. I'd pick one up, shake it and tell Charlie what was in it. Then he would label it immediately. As he opened the cases, Charlie was amazed to discover that I'd remembered exactly what was in each of them. Of course, Charlie improved on this system, if you can call it that, by marking the cases as soon as they were received.

Charles Stevenson brought a new orderliness to everything. He set a permanent standard for immaculate housekeeping throughout the company. And he taught us all better working habits. To this day when people comment on the efficiency of Hallmark, I immediately think of him.

Charlie used to say: "You get a job out on the table, and it's half done." He also made frequent notes on three-by-five-inch cards. That was another practice I adopted from Charlie — and that almost every executive in our company follows to this day.

By this time Charlie Stevenson was no longer resigning once a week for lack of work. He was supervising shipping, stock handling, manufacturing — and generally keeping things in order. We hired an accounting firm to establish costs for producing our cards. Until that time we set prices simply by comparing our cards with the competition and by past experience. Our equipment was crude by comparison with the larger manufacturers, but we continued to add graphic processes and were getting into a position to put more quality into our cards. As a result we began selling more and making a profit.

Everyday cards were becoming more prominent — that is, cards for births and birthdays, weddings and anniversaries, illnesses and expressions of sympathy. We expanded this line as well as our seasonal cards. And other seasons began to sell better — Halloween, St. Patrick's Day, Thanksgiving and Father's Day. Mother's Day was already well established by an act of Congress in 1914.

We introduced the custom of sending cards simply expressing friendship in 1919. There was no particular occasion associated with them, and it wasn't long before these became an important part of our line, adding cards with much deeper sentiments. Thanksgiving cards were new when we started the business in 1910. After World War I, we recognized their increasing popularity. At about the same time, congratulatory cards for weddings, births and anniversaries were coming into their own. Birthday cards carried general messages until we introduced lines expressly for a mother. These were followed by other specific sentiments for family members and friends.

Sometimes we have been credited with practically inventing greeting cards. However, it certainly can be said that we played a large role in popularizing them — and greatly enlarging the custom of sending them. But the history of the development of greeting cards is a study in itself. Ancient Egyptians sent greetings on papyrus; the Greeks used scrolls. And the Apostle Paul began his letters, "Grace to you and peace."

It was crucial to our future to get into the eastern market, especially New York, the most important in the country. A salesman in New York named Harry Lange was recommended to me, and I made an appointment to meet him.

There had been a smallpox epidemic in Kansas City that was so bad at one point no one was allowed to go out without a vaccination. I had one a few days before I left for New York, and it showed no signs of giving me any trouble until I got on the train. By the time I reached New York, my arm was inflamed and had a lump as big as a grapefruit.

I had a reservation at the old Waldorf-Astoria on Fifth Avenue and 34th Street — and what was reserved was the worst room I have ever seen in a good hotel in a large city. It wasn't much larger than my office and had no bathroom or windows. It was the only thing I could get since there was an automobile show in town and all the hotels were full.

Under these circumstances I met Harry Lange. He was a Brooklynite, complete with the accent and mannerisms. At first I didn't see the diamond for the rough. I didn't want him, and he didn't want me either. Still we decided to meet again the next day.

Even though I was terribly ill, things did look up because I was able to get a better room. I finally decided to take a chance on Harry and engaged him not only to cover New York City but the entire state as well. This was quite a territory for one man to handle. Today we have about seventy salesmen working it.

Harry was just the man for the job. New York buyers were tough, but Harry had the determination to hang on like a bulldog, smiling all the time, until he came out with the order. He proved that New York could be sold by a western manufacturer, which was not easy in those days. Harry's enthusiasm was contagious, and his integrity was beyond reproach. He was loyal to the company and his customers. And he knew his product as well as any man we have ever had and loved the greeting card business.

Through Harry we hired several excellent book salesmen, since that business was in a slump. Among them was Louis Westbrook, one of the finest men I've ever known. He opened up California for us. The same year, 1922, Charles B. Sefranka started with us as creative director. He was a great gentleman and served us well until his retirement in 1954. In 1922 we had sixteen salesmen doing business in all forty-eight states. Our staff in Kansas City had grown from four in 1911 to one hundred twenty in 1922.

The Denver Dry Goods Company was — and still is — one of the largest and finest department stores in the West. It was a key account which I started covering myself. Since I had no experience selling department stores, I figured this would be valuable to me. It was quite different from selling small merchants, where the buyer owns the store. In a department store a buyer reports to a merchandise manager who reports to a vice president. This experience taught me a great deal about how to expand our business. I continued to work Denver for about six years, until I couldn't take the time away from the office any longer. It was the last direct selling I ever had the opportunity to do.

We were expanding gradually when we were made an offer that would have doubled our business almost immediately. One of the largest retail operators in the country guaranteed us an annual volume of business about equal to what we were presently doing if, in return, we would give him a small discount. If we doubled our volume we would greatly reduce our costs by printing much larger runs. The profit from the additional business would have more than made up for the discount.

The offer came to Harry Lange in New York, and he considered it irresistible. In fact, I was alone in my reluctance to accept it. I felt that the business had been started on the principle of treating every customer the same, which meant one price to all with no concessions of any kind. Rejecting that offer was one of the toughest decisions I ever made — and just about the loneliest. Propositions of this sort came up several times again, and by then it was with some pride that we turned them down. This, of course, was well before the Robinson-Patman Act outlawed such practices in 1936.

Our business was growing faster than we could find trained personnel to keep it up. We started training people ourselves and soon gained a reputation that encouraged good people to come to us. Space again became a problem, and we rented a building across the street from our main operation. By this time we were in four separate locations. We began to wonder if moving into still more rented space was as economical as building a small factory of our own.

We took options on four pieces of property. The most desirable was at Twenty-sixth and Grand, about a mile from downtown Kansas City. We were concerned that our employees would consider this inconvenient, so we put the four locations to a vote. The result was strongly in favor of Twenty-sixth and Grand. We didn't think about it at the time, but many years later we were told that this was a revolutionary thing to do. We were dealing with personnel relations before that concern had even developed — and long before personnel departments became fixtures in American industry. The selection of that location proved a good one. Today Hallmark headquarters are just a block away and include this space and a great deal more.

Frank Hill Smith, who owned an architectural firm in Dayton, Ohio, estimated our building would cost $250,000. To get the building under roof, it was necessary to have loans from two banks on a ninety-nine-year lease. We were off to building a six-story factory, designed to add six more floors if needed. We were sure this would take care of us forever.

Charles S. Stevenson was hired by J.C. Hall as an order lister in 1919 following Stevenson's discharge from the army.

Evert Wampler lied about his age so he could be hired by Hall Brothers in 1915. He retired in 1967.

© Karsh, Ottawa

William P. Harsh, Sr., came to Hall Brothers in 1936 after graduating from the University of Missouri. He initiated many of the company's innovative personnel policies and practices. Harsh retired in 1976 and continues to serve as a consultant.

(Above right) C.E. "Ed" Goodman was executive vice president and a member of the board of directors when he retired in 1977 after forty-eight years of service to the company.

Charles B. Sefranka began working at Hall Brothers as creative director in 1922. He was with the company thirty-two years.

Hans Archenhold brought his extensive knowledge of lithography when he came to Hallmark from Germany in 1940. He continues to contribute as a consultant in the graphic arts field, having retired in 1970.

We moved into our new plant in July of 1923 and were plenty proud of it. But there was one serious handicap — no place to eat nearby except the Fred Harvey restaurant in Union Station, which was good but expensive. So we started our first company cafeteria. The cooking I had done as a youngster gave me enough understanding to train people to run it.

At this stage, we even had space to lease, which we did to an outfit that called itself an advertising company. Three young men ran the company, paying their rent with never a hitch. They seemed extremely industrious and received an enormous amount of mail — two or three full sacks a day — and they would send out just as much themselves.

This struck me as a little strange, but I paid no heed until a couple of years later when I learned that the three had been arrested for using the mails to defraud. It turned out that their business was a sort of holding company for a number of small outlets, each selling some mail-order gimmick for about a dollar apiece. One of the products they offered was an aluminum strip, folded in such a way that it would slip into the ear to amplify hearing. They also advertised a bottle of some sort of bluing that was guaranteed to prevent bedwetting. The only other item I remember was even more ridiculous. It was a bug exterminator, which you would expect to be a liquid, but it was simply a block of wood on which you placed the bug and, I guess, stomped it.

After their arrest we decided to look over the operation. There were a dozen large mail sacks, each with as many as a thousand letters presumably containing a dollar bill or more. The court made arrangements to have these returned to the senders — but there had been a lot of people over the years who had bought a dollar's worth of blue sky. The three men were sentenced to prison terms at Leavenworth. Still, I remember them as being as fine a looking bunch of fellows as I have ever seen.

I had great affection for my old rolltop desk, but it just didn't fit with the modern furniture and equipment in our new plant. I went to the largest office supply company in town to look at desks. A salesman showed me a fine flat-topped walnut desk that was bigger than the one I had. He said the desk had belonged to an Indian in Tulsa who had struck oil on his land. The Indian could neither read nor write. The only use he made of the desk was to sit with his feet on top of it, with one of the drawers filled with sawdust to use as a cuspidor. He had stopped making

80

payments on the desk, and I bought it for the balance due. I used it until we moved again thirteen years later. It seems I have rated a new desk every time we've changed locations.

By this time my brother Bill had sold his book and stationery store in Norfolk, Nebraska, and come to Kansas City with his family. He joined Rollie and me as office manager and treasurer, expanding Hall Brothers to three. Within a few years we were using all the space in our building as well as leasing an adjoining one. We had come a long way from my twelve-by-twelve-foot room in the YMCA to a building of our own with sixty thousand square feet.

On Halloween when witches fly
Riding broomsticks through the sky
May all the craft they know be spent
Finding you heaps of merriment.

Hits and Misses

Not many years ago an English history professor, C. Northcote Parkinson, wrote a humorous book called *Parkinson's Law*. He showed that as the British navy increased its personnel, it lessened its efficiency. Parkinson explained: "Work expands so as to fill the time available for its completion."

Parkinson's Law also demonstrated that as one man saw another doing similar work with a secretary to help him, he would create more work in order to justify a secretary for himself. To keep her busy, he required an assistant. The assistant, to prove his importance, would introduce more systems and records, making it necessary for him to have a separate secretary. At that point it took all the top man's time to check their work. As a result he had to farm out some of the checking, which required an additional assistant — and so on and on. Parkinson's book applied so appropriately to modern business behavior that it found a ready market in America.

Our business proved to be fertile ground for Parkinson's Law. At the time, we were making about six hundred different items a year. Each item was basically an individual design and had to be redesigned every year. (Today we produce about fourteen thousand new designs a year.) A consulting engineer looked over our operation and said that it was the most complicated business he had ever seen. He pointed out that most businesses introduce a product and stay with it for years without significant changes. We began to feel the need for more effective systems and records. And as we introduced them, our people felt all their problems would be solved.

Charlie Stevenson was a very practical fellow who just wanted to get the job done — and I certainly shared this feeling. A couple of times a year we would review all these systems and records to see how many we could eliminate without interrupting normal procedures. We approached them on a theory I had long held — that there is a simpler and better way to do everything.

We thought perhaps we could simplify procedures by combining

82

them. We hired an efficiency expert to create a schedule board for us. It was very costly, and the most organized-looking thing I had ever seen. But it had one great fault — it didn't work. It took more people to run the thing than it had taken to do the entire scheduling job.

That's when Charlie adopted a system of his own. A railing about ten inches wide ran around his office. When we had a line of cards to get out, Charlie would arrange samples on the railing. We'd sort out the cards that weren't moving through production fast enough and get them going. This worked when the company was small; now it takes a staff of experts and a battery of computers to do the job.

Charlie made a great contribution to our business. He was my right-hand man — running production, shipping and property management. He became our general manager and stayed with the company forty-one years until his retirement in 1960.

We outgrew our new building in less than two years. We leased additional space, and by 1929 we occupied seventy-five thousand square feet. As we added more people I became concerned about improving our hiring practices. One night I went to a lecture, sitting in the front row with several people I knew well. The speaker was a character analyst. He started sizing up the people in our group, and I was amazed by his accuracy.

After the speech I tried to make a deal with him to screen job applicants for us. He didn't have the time, he said, "But I've got a girl who can do it — my assistant." Her name was Grace Shuey. Before hiring her, I had her analyze people who were already working for us — and she was quite accurate. She joined us full time to judge applicants for jobs.

We prepared a form which she'd fill out during an interview; then she'd rate the applicant. She could tell if an individual was bright or lazy or ambitious, but her system failed to show much about character weaknesses. It soon became apparent that it wasn't working. Even though she had a contract with us, she admitted she wasn't doing us much good, and to her credit she left.

One of the most frequent mistakes made in hiring people is to confuse ability and affability. Now affability is a wonderful trait, but if it's not accompanied by ability, it doesn't amount to much. Of course, it is extremely important to sell yourself. People have to believe in you and get along with you. But if your opinions are contrary to theirs, you've got to have the courage to say so whether it's popular or not.

Employees at Hall Brothers picnics; above, 1921; below, 1925

(Overleaf) *Sales personnel in Crown Room during 1959 Sales Conference*

Early employee card shop

Present-day employee card shop

Hall Brothers Amateur Follies, 1938

The Noon News, *a daily employee newspaper, was first published in 1927*

The first company cafeteria

Crown Room in the headquarters building

I also think an excellent employee will work harder for rewards other than money. He'll put a sense of accomplishment first — and the money will take care of itself. If you show a well-intentioned individual just what to do and set a good example yourself, he'll get along just fine. A more difficult lesson, and one that took a little longer for me to learn is: the sooner we get rid of someone who makes no effort to do a good job, the better. However, I always found that talking about this idea was much easier than executing it.

As a boy I had read an article about R. H. Macy's program of hiring and training people, and I continued to read about Macy's employment practices. They inspired me as our business grew. Macy's was one of the leaders in developing policies — such as training programs — that led to successful personnel operations.

Time and again I was told that large industries hired people for as little money as possible and worked them as hard as they could. Little consideration was given when people were ill. The belief was prevalent that treating people too well spoiled them.

In this regard I often found myself in disagreement with our supervisors. One night I had two extra tickets to the theater. I suggested to the office manager that we give them to someone who had been doing a particularly good job. He felt it would only spoil the person who received them and suggested I give them to a relative or friend, which I did reluctantly. I was irked with myself for this decision.

Shortly after that, I had a long visit with my next-door neighbor, Joe Dawson, who taught me an important lesson in handling people. Joe had retired after many years of supervising people at the Wells Fargo Express Company. He found that established practices of constantly watching over people and reprimanding them for the slightest infraction were not productive. The best results were obtained by simply treating people decently and expecting the same in return.

Our personnel practices continued to improve and to be innovative. And probably the man who did the most in setting these standards was William P. Harsh. I hired him in 1936 just out of the University of Missouri, where he lettered in football. Bill was a man who perfectly combined ability and affability. We lost him to the navy during the war, but he returned in 1945 and became personnel director in 1947.

Bill Harsh makes more friends in less time than anybody I have ever known — and keeps them. He never forgets a name and is forever doing things for people that endear him to them. He simply likes people and they know it — perhaps that's what "personnel" is all about. His philosophy fit right in with our company. We simply felt that doing a little better by our people than they expected not only gave us great satisfaction but was good business as well.

We were one of the first companies of any size to introduce bonuses for employees. As early as 1927, each employee received ten dollars for every year he had been with the company. The federal government declared a "Victory Tax" in 1943, which lead to tax withholding. To soften the blow, we paid everyone who had worked a year or more an extra week's salary as an income tax bonus. We continued to experiment with bonus plans over the years. For example, in 1956 when we moved into our new headquarters, an "Appreciation Bonus" of fifty dollars for each year of service, up to $250, was given.

In addition to bonuses, as early as 1935, Charles Stevenson outlined more than twenty proposals for personnel benefits that were virtually unknown in industry — especially at a time when just getting any kind of a job at all was the problem for millions of Americans. The program included a retirement pension, medical aid, life insurance and vacation pay.

In 1956 Bill Harsh proposed an extension of these benefits and added an ambitious Career Rewards Program that included life, accident and medical insurance; profit sharing; a savings program with high interest; a new retirement plan with an early-age provision; and extensive educational assistance. *Fortune* magazine called the package "the country's most liberal employee-benefit and profit-sharing plan."

In 1924 we introduced two unusual ideas for greeting cards that might be described as "a hit and a miss." The hit was a line of nonfolding "flat cards." They were made by laminating three sheets of heavy paper together, then stamping on steel-die presses in gold and black. The remaining coloring was done by hand. We lined the envelopes with heavy gold foil and used our best sentiments on them — including Edgar Guest's "My Friend." The cards were five inches by six inches, a good size for a quality card, and sold for twenty-five cents.

People liked these flat cards better than anything else on the market at the time. Dealers bought them in quantities, and they were in the best stores in the country. Their success encouraged my belief that the public wanted quality products, especially in greeting cards that reflect the personality and taste of the sender. These cards were at their peak about 1928 when we ran a full-page advertisement in *Ladies' Home Journal* — our first fling in national advertising.

The same year we brought out the flat cards, a manufacturer of plastic phonograph records came to us with the idea of sending greetings on them. We could record an eight-line sentiment with a musical background. We were told that the idea couldn't be patented, and if we wanted to be first on the market, we'd have to move fast — other plastics manufacturers were offering the idea to our competitors. We rushed out a line of records called "Greetaphones" mounted on quality cards. We were so confident of their success that we sent a shipment to every good dealer we had with the promise that if they didn't sell, he could return them.

They were a disaster. The records, about two and one-half inches across, were almost impossible to understand unless you were familiar with the sentiments being read, as we were. Customers returned them to dealers demanding their money back. The dealers shipped them back to us for credit. We lost eighty thousand dollars; but worse, we lost considerable face with our dealers. However, we probably received a million dollars' worth of wisdom and made no other serious mistakes until 1932 — and that was a lulu.

A wholesale florist came to us with an idea that seemed to have great potential. It was a small block of peat moss with a coating of melted asphalt containing three or four lily-of-the-valley bulbs. The peat moss was moistened, and when the bulbs were brought to room temperature they would sprout and bloom. He had marketed them for Christmas the year before in a few big stores, keeping them under refrigeration until they were ready to be sold. They had been a phenomenal success selling for a dollar each.

We designed a container shaped like a flowerpot and called them "Wunderflowers." The dealers were enthusiastic and ordered thousands of them. We even arranged for cold storage in all the principal cities and made sure they reached the warehouses in plenty of time for Christmas. We informed our dealers that Wunderflowers had to be kept cool and only a few at a time should be brought out for display.

When the holiday rush began, dealers reordered them in large quantities to be delivered directly to their stockrooms. After a few days of warmth, the bulbs began to sprout right through the packages. Most of them had sprouted by the middle of December — and it was a mess.

Even though we had given sufficient warnings to dealers, there was nothing we could do but allow them credit. We suggested they send the flowers to children's hospitals, orphan homes and homes for the aged. We took a terrific loss, much greater than the Greetaphone cards. But, once again, we gained considerable good will with our dealers by accepting the full responsibility for the catastrophe.

These setbacks could have broken the company, but we were able to ride them out largely because they firmed up our dealers' faith in Hallmark. We became more cautious than ever about quick-buck merchandising schemes. From then on we would painstakingly examine every new idea before making a commitment. These experiences also prepared us for one of the most tempting offers we would ever receive.

Over the years we have had many offers to merge. I always felt that we didn't start our business to see how much money we could make, but to see how good a job we could do — and that is still our primary objective.

The first offer, which came in 1925, was a tough one to turn down — partly because it *was* the first. It came from a man I respected more than anyone else in the business, Arthur Eaton, chairman of the board of Eaton, Crane and Pike, a magical name to me in the stationery field especially. When we first started in business, Eaton shipped on credit the cards and envelopes we needed to manufacture our Christmas line. He didn't bill us until after the first of December when money from our sales would be coming in. I was also flattered that Eaton had consulted me on proposals that had come up within his own organization. On one, I had disagreed with his son, Colonel William Eaton, and was certain that would hurt my standing with the company. But it was Colonel Eaton who called to say that his father wanted to see me in Kansas City. I was terrifically pleased.

Arthur and William Eaton wanted to discuss a merger of our companies. Our joint sales force could sell their lines as well as ours. They had a

"Wunderflowers," a 1932 greeting that was intended to sprout at Christmas — but only if bulbs were kept in a refrigerated stockroom. Dealers put them in normal storage areas and were faced with large quantities of lilies-of-the-valley. Dealers were credited.

As your customer receives it   After one week   After two weeks   After three weeks — in full bloom

In 1928 Joyce Hall designed this full-page advertisement for Ladies' Home Journal, Hall Brother's first national advertising

(Below) A typical Christmas card with a sentiment written especially for "Mother."

Merry Christmas Mother

Dear Mother mine with heart of gold
May gifts from up above
And earthly blessings manifold
Reward you for your love

In 1924 Hall Brothers introduced "Greetaphones," a flat card with a phonograph record attached. Unfortunately the recordings were almost impossible to understand and dealers had to be credited.

large building available where our greeting card plant could operate. They had investigated our financial situation and proposed a liberal stock arrangement. Eaton would continue as chairman and his son as president of the papeterie division. I would be executive vice president, overseeing the greeting card operation. This sounded like moving into the big time very rapidly, and I was scared. I could think of little else except the glory and prestige that would go with being an executive officer of Eaton, Crane and Pike with offices in a vine-covered building in Massachusetts and a New York office two hours away by train.

After a month had passed, the glamour of the offer began to wear thin. I'd started thinking again about some of the things we had hoped to accomplish ourselves. Finally, with the consent of my brothers, I called Mr. Eaton, thanked him for the confidence he had shown in us and said that we had decided to stay on our own in Kansas City. We continued to buy paper from them in increasing volume for several years.

A number of changes had taken place in the stationery industry. It had been curtailed by the rapidly growing greeting card business. We made thank-you notes and were continually pressured by dealers and salesmen to make a line of writing paper. However, as long as the Eatons had an interest in the same business, we didn't want to be in competition. That was the measure of my respect for them.

The Eaton, Crane and Pike proposal did give us pause in regard to our location. By 1926 our business was primarily in the West, while our competition was practically all in the East — and eastern dealers were not accustomed to buying merchandise from western manufacturers. We seriously considered moving East. Elizabeth and I made an exploratory trip through all the major cities from Massachusetts to Virginia. We learned some things we didn't know before — like the difficulties of manufacturing in these concentrated population centers. Manufacturers were beginning to move to the South and Midwest, and the Pacific Coast was developing as well.

Back in Kansas City, our business was showing large increases. It was necessary again to lease additional space. We had built an organization that we felt we'd have a hard time duplicating anywhere else. We fully realized the importance of the quality of the environment and the people in making quality products. We decided then that we had the best location in the industry. Our roots now were firmly in Kansas City, and this is a decision we have never regretted.

W e had been operating a retail store in Chicago for several years on a profitable basis. In 1928, when our lease was about to expire, we were notified that we would not be able to renew it. The building was to be torn down.

We had a real estate man canvass every location on Michigan Avenue. He was able to turn up a one-hundred-foot frontage a few doors from our store. It belonged to the Stanley McCormick estate. Since we only needed twenty-five feet, we could sublease the remaining space with the consent of the lessor — "which permission should not be unreasonably withheld." It was a phrase I would never forget.

The agents for the McCormick estate told us they had an offer from a candy and catering firm for forty feet of the space. We got busy trying to lease the other twenty and soon found a milliner who wanted it. We signed a lease for fifteen years and drew leases with the candy firm and the milliner. When we presented the package to the McCormick people, they informed us they no longer represented the estate. A conservator had taken over.

We went to see him with every confidence that our leases would be accepted. We were stunned when he said he could not accept the sublease for the candy company because there was a similar operation in the Mary McCormick Building just a few doors from ours. The conservator represented both McCormick interests.

It was October, 1929. Before we could complete another arrangement, the last of October rolled around — and with it the stock market crash.

The milliner's lease had the same clause as ours — that he could sublease with our permission. But the tenant he had lined up was not acceptable to the conservator; so we had to refuse permission. With the crash, all interest in leasing real estate was gone. The milliner sued us for withholding permission from him to sublease. Since it was really the McCormick estate that had refused him, there was nothing for us to do but sue the estate on the same basis.

There seemed little chance to win both cases, but we did feel we'd win one since the circumstances were identical. However, they were tried by different judges — and we lost both ways. This left us with the entire property back on our hands. There was nothing to do but negotiate a settlement with the McCormick estate through the conservator.

He was a trust officer of a large Chicago bank. When I called on him, he was most cordial. He said, "Sit down, Hall." He looked me over and said, "You know, I think I'm going to like you when I get to know you. You're in a bad spot, and I'm sorry I've got this job. But I have to negotiate this in the best interest of my client. Before this is over, I may have to take the shirt off your back. But I promise you one thing, I'll do it like a gentleman."

We had many interviews after that — in fact, in one year's time I made seventy-five round trips on the Santa Fe between Chicago and Kansas City. I spent three nights a week on the train, and about the only thing I got out of it was the friendship of every conductor, brakeman, porter and waiter on the line.

When we finally worked out a settlement, he *had* just about taken the shirt off my back. In losing these actions, we had suffered our own private crash and had no need for the entire economy of the country to come down on us as well. We were hit as hard as anyone during the Depression, probably harder, because no one had had any experience with what happened to greeting cards in bad times.

Of course, almost everyone decided that people would stop buying greeting cards. But I wasn't sure this would be the case. Perhaps people would be even more concerned about communicating with one another. I felt there might even be a greater demand for greeting cards. People would buy them as acceptable substitutes for gifts.

Though business had increased steadily, by 1932 confidence in the economy was so low that we were having trouble collecting our bills. We were frightened, but not panicked. And against the advice of almost everyone concerned, I refused to lay off a single employee. Finally, we did have to make two ten-percent salary cuts, but it wasn't long before we restored full pay.

I had seen enough ups and downs in the building of the business that I was sure there was a solution to this crisis, too. I proposed a basic plan to fight the Depression. Businesses were buying only what they needed for immediate use. I asked our suppliers and customers to anticipate their needs for at least a month in advance so they could keep their people working. In return we would invest in future delivery for the next six months.

The plan worked well enough that Rotary International asked me to present it to its members. Rotary Clubs around the country began promoting it. W. H. Eaton recommended it to President Hoover's unemployment commission. As the plan caught on, more and more people were brought back to work, even if only part time. The newspapers began referring to the idea as the Hall Plan and crediting it with aiding recovery.

Finally the economy got into such desperate shape that even if every business had adopted the plan, it could not have saved the situation. After President Franklin D. Roosevelt came to office in 1933, closing the banks and making other dramatic efforts to get the economy moving again, the situation began to improve.

Congress passed President Roosevelt's National Recovery Act, which required every industry to write a code for its operation. As president of the Greeting Card Association, I appointed a committee to draw up a code. The central issue was allowing western manufacturers to maintain stockrooms in New York City. This was crucial to our business since we couldn't properly service the East without carrying stock in the area.

The committee represented three sections of the country — one man from the East, one from Ohio and one from Illinois. The Illinois man presented the case for us so effectively that it was easily approved. However, when the revised code was submitted to the membership by the board, it contained a clause prohibiting the New York stockrooms. The Illinois man had changed his mind, and the Ohio man voted with him. The clause was approved by the entire association. It turned out that the Illinois man was taking an executive position with the Ohio firm. The Depression was problem enough without losing our competitive position in the East.

General Hugh S. Johnson, Administrator of the NRA, had come to Kansas City on other business, and he agreed to meet with me while he was in town. He couldn't see me until nine in the evening. When I arrived, he was entertaining some of his local business friends, and it was apparent they were having a good time, including his secretary, who was serving cocktails. By the time I got to see the general, I doubted that I'd have any influence under these circumstances, or even if I did, that he'd remember the next day.

The general, who was from Oklahoma, asked a few questions, then said, "Mr. Hall, those easterners aren't going to put anything over on us. I assure you that if that clause is left in the code when it's presented to me, it'll be thrown out."

The party continued to flourish, and as I left, I figured he'd forget all about my problem. However, a week later a letter arrived from the general restating his position. I went to the annual meeting of the association armed with this letter. I didn't say a word about it, but continued to argue the principle, feeling that I had an ace in the hole. I never had to use it, because the code never reached General Johnson's office. The NRA was declared unconstitutional. Just the same, I was forever grateful to General Johnson, a fair and tough-minded gentleman.

In making regular trips to our territories, I became increasingly aware that the single greatest handicap we had in selling greeting cards was the way they were displayed. Some stores put them on the top of showcases in the cardboard shipping boxes. Others kept them in drawers, and the customers had to ask to see them. Cards would often be sitting out on counters, exposed to light and dust the year round. More progressive dealers used metal racks to display cards, and a few had carpenters build wooden ones. These were somewhat better, but no one had come up with any real solution.

In the late twenties I remember standing on the mezzanine of a large department store looking down on the first floor, which had just been refurnished with new showcases. Greeting cards made the poorest showing of any merchandise there. I determined then that something dramatic had to be done about displaying cards.

In 1935 an architectural designer was hired to work on ideas for a walnut display fixture to show greeting cards in the open where people could see them and get at them freely. We felt the fixture should sit on a base with rows of shelves at eye level. The shelves should vary in slant from bottom to top to hold cards at a natural reading angle, and lighting should be built into the fixture. A design was developed and patented.

A program was announced to sell walnut display fixtures at cost to our dealers. No one in the industry, including our own organization, believed dealers would buy them. And for the first few months it looked as if they were right. The salesmen had to use photographs to show the fixtures, which was a great disadvantage.

Then I heard about a salesman who was doing a successful job of showing women's dresses in a converted house trailer attached to the back of his car. Trailers were new and created great interest. We had a good-looking trailer built and installed the fixtures with a model display of greeting cards. It was sent over the territories to show dealers firsthand what they would be buying. This was somewhat better but was still not selling many fixtures.

A young man, C. E. "Ed" Goodman, who had started with us in 1929, was in charge of our dealers' service program. We decided that someone who enthusiastically believed in the importance of these fixtures could sell them. Ed took a trailer on the road himself, and it wasn't long before we sent out a fleet of trailers around the country. By 1939 the trailers were discontinued — the fixtures were selling themselves. After installing them, dealers soon learned that business didn't just increase, it doubled or tripled — so they kept adding to their original installations.

Ed Goodman made many significant contributions to the company. In 1955 he became executive vice president and was on our board of directors until he retired in 1977.

The importance of the introduction of display fixtures cannot be overestimated. They represented another turning point in the overall success of the greeting card industry. The rest of the industry followed our example, copying our fixtures as closely as possible without infringing on our patent. Today almost all greeting cards are sold from fixtures that aren't much different in concept from the first ones we designed over forty years ago. Fixtures also influenced the development of a totally new inventory system.

In the early days dealers bought from many small manufacturers and stocked more greeting cards than they really needed. At the same time, they didn't always have the right cards for their customers. Because of our experience with retail records, we were able to create a balanced line of cards with a stock control system. This new approach to controlling a line of cards was an extremely intricate job. We could give a dealer the cards that would sell best, and the system also insured that cards for specific occasions were always in stock.

Today these inventory decisions are made automatically — and more accurately — by computer. It not only keeps a record of everything we

(Opposite)
*Typical 1970's exterior
and interior design*

Rail car used in mid-thirties to deliver new fixtures

Trailers went on the road in 1936 to introduce dealers to new fixture design

This display fixture, designed by Hall Brothers in 1936, featured lighted, eye-level display of greeting cards. The design revolutionized the greeting card industry.

102

make, but also every card we have on fixtures in the stores we service around the globe. The dealer sends us computerized records of each card he wishes to reorder and gets back the same card or a replacement that has proven to have greater appeal.

With the success of display fixtures and our reorder system, once again we found ourselves needing more space. I began looking out my window at the huge Overland Building just north of us and dreaming of moving there. In 1936, shortly before the end of the year, I went to see a prominent local banker to inquire about the building. I was sure nothing would come of it.

On New Year's Eve our family was about to set off on a long overdue vacation in Florida. We were packed and ready to go. The telephone rang — it was the banker. He said, "Joyce, have you ever worked on New Year's Day?" He had talked with the owners of the building, and apparently it was an opportune time to meet with them. It didn't take me long to agree, although I hated to disappoint the children. (We made the trip a few weeks later.)

We bought the Overland Building for about a fifth of what it had cost to build it in 1919. It had six stories with 240,000 square feet, which came close to doubling the space we occupied. We now had almost eight hundred employees, and surely enough space for any future expansion. Just the same, I started buying the land adjoining the building.

Charlie Stevenson moved into the building first to plan the transfer of employees and equipment. He'd drive his car onto the big freight elevator, ride to the fourth floor and park right in front of his desk. (The solid masonry building had originally been designed for automobile storage.) Each employee was given a card with a number and instructions. When he came to work in the new plant, the card directed him to his department without a moment lost. It was the smoothest move I'd ever seen.

We remembered what had happened when we moved into our new plant in 1923 — there was a general letdown in production. Much to our surprise, the new equipment and spacious surroundings had a curious psychological effect — that somehow all this would do the job for us. Manufacturing costs went up along with other expenses. It took several months for everyone to get down to business. We were determined not to

104

let this happen again. But we went through the same difficulties after moving into the Overland Building. And this happened again following the move into the headquarters we now occupy.

Variations of this best-selling card have been in the Hallmark line continuously since 1942.

The Crowning Glory

As a manufacturer of greeting cards, I had always felt that part of my job was to check out the merchandising methods of stores around the country. We were planning a new retail store in Kansas City and wanted to show how well greeting cards could be displayed along with a variety of other merchandise. It would also give us a chance to experiment with new Hallmark products.

Late in 1949, I came across a story in *Time* magazine about a new Bullock's store in Pasadena, California, that had been designed by the architectural firm of Wurdeman & Becket. It impressed me that before starting their plans the architects had set up an office in an established Bullock's store to study the operation. On a trip to Los Angeles I visited the new Bullock's and was so fascinated I spent the entire day looking around. It had a completely new interior style that glorified the merchandise and not just the store.

The design of our store had been completed, and it would delay our opening several months if we changed it. Just the same, I made an appointment with Wurdeman & Becket to discuss an entirely new interior for our store. They made a convincing presentation on how they would handle it. Of course, this meant paying their fee in addition to the investment we had already made. As usual with any building project, it took longer to complete than expected. We didn't move in until December 1, 1950, a serious handicap to our holiday business. But we all felt it had been worth the delay and additional cost.

We were also planning an addition to our plant that presented a number of problems. It would have to be built in the parking lot adjoining it — but we needed more parking space, not less. There was a sizeable parcel of land nearby that we hadn't given much thought to because most of it was a rocky hill that rose several stories above street level. It amounted to seven acres divided among forty different owners. We got options for all of it.

It occurred to me that it might be possible to build our addition on top of the hill and connect it to the old plant by a bridge over the street — if the city would allow it. I hesitated to propose this to the architects. But after Welton Becket studied the site, he said, "Joyce, this is the place to build your addition." The new building could be connected to the old by an elevated passageway. Becket designed a much larger plant than we could have built on the parking lot, which gave us room for expansion.

In 1956 we moved into our new headquarters. The city permitted us to build a two-level, enclosed bridge thirty feet above a busy street. The building is nestled into the hill with a small first floor that is level with the second floor of our existing plant, the Overland Building. As a result, it is the shape of an irregular, inverted pyramid rising to eight stories. While the first floor is only 7,000 square feet, the largest floor — the seventh — contains about 200,000 square feet. Later we added a ninth floor and a penthouse with a guest apartment.

We considered the environment of the new plant just as crucial as the design. Greeting cards represent thoughtfulness, and it's fitting that those who create them should be working in the best conditions we could provide. The day we moved into the new building — which everyone called "Cross Over the Bridge" from a popular song — I noticed that our people were a little better dressed. The women had their hair done, and the men had their shoes shined. In all our plants we had strived to create conditions that influenced people for the best — not only in the quality of their work but their appearance as well.

There are comfortable lounge areas throughout the building where employees can visit and relax on coffee breaks. Our walls are decorated with paintings, murals and sculptures representing one of the largest private art collections in the country. And we frequently have changing exhibits in addition to a permanent display of the paintings of Sir Winston Churchill, Norman Rockwell, Grandma Moses, Salvador Dali, Edward Hopper and Saul Steinberg.

Certainly one of our proudest pieces of art is in the reception room to my office. One morning shortly after we moved in, I was mysteriously asked to appear outside my office. An exquisite Steuben fountain had been placed there as a gift from Hallmark employees in appreciation of the new working conditions. What touched me most was that it had been financed through hundreds of small contributions.

Most people despair of company cafeterias — usually for good reason. In our new headquarters, we established the Crown Room, which is

Y. M. C. A. Building,
Kansas City, Mo.

*Having outgrown the mail facilities and
storage at the "Y," Hall rented space in the
Braley Building*

*In 1915 the company moved to the
second floor of the Starr Piano Company
at Eleventh Street and Grand Avenue*

Hall
BRO'S

HALL MARK CARDS

first building designed and built especially for Hall Brothers in 1923

B ROTHERS

A HALLMARK CARD

In 1936 the company refurbished the larger Overland Building
at Twenty-fifth Street and Grand Avenue

Hallmark Cards

The present international headquarters of Hallmark Cards is located only a block from the site of the first building built by Hall Brothers in 1922. This building, occupied in 1956 and having undergone many expansions and rennovations, was designed by Welton Becket. Constructed against a rock hillside, the building is an inverted pyramid with the first floor so small it occupies little more than the entrance lobby and elevators. The building is unique in that it was designed to fit the contours of the land as well as accommodate the growing industry it would house.

J.C. Hall studying the architect's rendering of the new corporate headquarters occupied in 1956. Shown at right, with additions, as it now appears.

decorative and surrounded by windows with expansive views. We have tried to serve food in all our plants that is as good as the finest restaurants. In a recent competition with the best industrial and public restaurants in the Midwest, the Crown Room won the most prizes — three firsts and two seconds.

As we introduced new products, we began thinking about a really fine showcase store that would sell only Hallmark merchandise. Of course, it had to be in New York, and our first choice for a location was Fifth Avenue and Fifty-sixth Street, where three corners were occupied by Bonwit Teller, Steuben Glass and Harry Winston, Inc., the famous diamond store.

After several turndowns on acquiring this location, we finally got a lease for the northwest corner. It was a fifty-foot front, one hundred feet deep, with a full basement. We felt that half of this would be plenty of room, and we could sublease the rest. Then I asked Henry Dreyfuss, the industrial designer and consultant to Hallmark, to look at the space. He immediately said we should take the entire fifty feet and the basement, using the additional space for a gallery.

We wanted architect Edward Durrell Stone to design the store. When I mentioned this to one knowledgeable New Yorker, he laughed and said that Stone didn't design little retail stores — he designed General Motors buildings and U. S. embassies. I visited Ed Stone, and we became good friends. All I told him was to make the store the best looking shop on Fifth Avenue, and he liked the challenge.

Stone's solution for the gallery was to cut back the first floor sixteen feet, exposing the lower level to the street through huge arched windows. The exterior is of travertine marble. The Fifth Avenue Association gave the store its coveted architectural award.

There are many galleries in New York showing fine art, but we wanted people to see the arts of everyday life — the so-called "unsophisticated arts." One exhibit, called "Wildflowers," had a forest of living trees, shrubs, flowers and a real waterfall. Another was a full-sized wine cellar complete with cobwebs. Then we turned the gallery into a playground where visitors could take part in a variety of games. We had biographical exhibits honoring many notable figures and special Christmas shows that were always the

112

most popular. Recently, as our product lines continued to expand, we have used the lower level as an extension of our retail space.

The store, which opened in June, 1964, has proven to be a great international showcase on probably the best corner of the most important and highest quality shopping street in America — and perhaps in the world.

Jack Kaiser, president of our store in downtown Kansas City, made a persuasive presentation for a major new retail outlet in the city's Country Club Plaza shopping district. He argued that the downtown area had depreciated so badly that we needed a prestigious store in Kansas City's favorite shopping area. It seemed too ambitious to consider the same year we were opening the gallery. But Jack had all the right answers at the tip of his tongue.

Halls Plaza was designed by Paul Lazlo and Associates of Los Angeles with the able guidance of Henry Dreyfuss. Edward Durrell Stone advised us on both exterior and interior design. We thought it would be some time before the store would break even, let alone make a profit, but it proved a good example of the rewards of doing a quality job of retailing. In a short time, the store was profitable and has been ever since.

As far back as 1936, we began buying property adjacent to our main plant so we wouldn't wake up some morning with an undesirable operation in front of us. The first parcel was a block-long lot across the street. On another side there was a triangular lot, two blocks wide at the north, tapering south two blocks to a point. It was almost solid rock and was known in the city as Signboard Hill. In the early days a creek had run along the east side of the hill, and sometime in the late 1800's there had been a beer garden on the top called Tivoli. Signboard Hill, literally covered with signboards, was a real eyesore, especially with the beautiful Liberty Memorial building on the west and the Union Station across the street.

When we built our new headquarters, connected to our existing plant, in 1955, Signboard Hill became a threat to our entire complex. The principal owners of Signboard Hill were holding on to the property until someone wanted to build on it. In 1958 a buyer came along who planned to build a popular-priced motel on the hill. We had our archi-

Hallmark Gallery

Hallmark Gallery, Fifth Avenue at 56th Street, New York City

(Above) *"The Art of the Wedding" exhibition dealt with the symbols and customs of weddings around the world*

(Bottom) *A retrospective exhibition of photographs by Harry Callahan was held in 1964*

Halls on the Plaza, Kansas City

Exterior, Above, and Interior, Left, of Halls at Crown Center, Kansas City

tect, Welton Becket, look it over. He reported that it was one of the best sites for a hotel he had ever seen. We bought it, determined to save it for a first-class hotel, something Kansas City needed badly.

We continued to acquire other property in the vicinity so we would have some control of what would be built around us. Before long we were in the real estate business and wondered what we should do about it. Like so many American cities, downtown Kansas City suffered while the suburban areas blossomed with huge shopping complexes.

We are located about midway between the heart of the downtown and the Country Club Plaza — seven minutes from the Plaza and five minutes from downtown by way of Grand Avenue, a wide and handsome thoroughfare. Colonel William Rockhill Nelson and his *Kansas City Star* were boosting Grand Avenue when I came to town in 1910. I believed he was right then — and I still do. Our property bridged the downtown district at one end and the Plaza, and we felt that our property could be developed to enhance the fortunes of both.

In 1966, our headquarters neighborhood consisted mainly of used-car lots, light industry, small businesses, old warehouses, vacant buildings and a few family residences. But bordering on these less attractive areas were historic Union Cemetery, Penn Valley Park and Liberty Memorial Park. Here was the potential to develop a controlled residential and commercial environment that would literally be surrounded by parks. Furthermore, we felt we could do something for the city that had done so much for us.

After several years of studying and planning, we concluded that we wanted to build a total urban complex. And a decade after that dream had first taken shape, a formal plan for its creation was approved by the city council. We decided to call the complex Crown Center, relating to the symbol of Hallmark.

The first ground-breaking ceremony took place in 1968, beginning a long construction program that will not be completed until the late 1980's. It was quite an event in the city, and civic officials joined Donald and me in turning the first shovels of dirt. This $400 million development would forever change eighty-five acres just twelve blocks south of the heart of the city.

We had determined throughout a decade of planning that everything would be of the highest quality. We intended for Crown Center to stand as a prime example of how private industry can contribute to the rebirth of this nation's inner cities. It is our hope that other companies in other cities will look first to their historic locations before relocating to the meadows and fields of the suburbs.

The architectural planning of Crown Center has been aimed at bringing people and their families back to the city. In a setting of landscaped plazas and walkways, gardens and fountains, Crown Center has four large office complexes; two major hotels; a large retail center; an international marketplace; a variety of fine restaurants; high-rise garden apartments and condominiums. There are cultural attractions and entertainment for the people of the area, plus a special section for children.

So far, things have gone well and according to our plan. Underground parking connects the total complex and makes getting around easy in bad weather. The outdoor events in the Central Square have been as diverse as kite-flying contests, folk music, ice skating, art fairs, marathons and highly-successful ethnic festivals put on by the Greek, Mexican, Jewish, Italian, Filipino and Black communities of Kansas City.

The neighborhood we moved to in 1922 is greatly changed today because of Crown Center, and thousands of people — including five thousand of our own employees — have a wholly revitalized "downtown suburb" for their work address. Donald and I knew all along that if people have an in-town environment they can be proud of, they will return to the heart of the city to live and work.

From the very beginning we knew we were going to need expert help. Folks say we do a pretty fair job of designing greeting cards, but engineering skyscrapers and running an efficient hotel have not been company specialties.

Before 1960, we had visited with Victor Gruen and Larry Smith about land use and the feasibility studies. The work of the firms headed by these two men started us in the right manner and the right direction.

The first visible results appeared in 1970 and 1971 when an office complex was completed with its vast underground garage and classic square with fountain. These were designed by Edward Larrabee Barnes of New York. Ed had been selected as our master planner, coordinating architect, and design architect for the first key buildings. He gave Crown Center a strong and sophisticated architectural style that has earned him justified praise across the country. His first building is a skyscraper on its side, a single structure with five interconnected, seven-story office buildings. Offices overlook the central square with its fountain, ice skating rink and landscaped terraces. Donald has further graced the area with large sculptures by Alexander Calder and David Smith, since modern sculpture is a special interest of his.

These offices opened in 1971, and I awaited the opening of the retail center. I have long studied good retailing and wanted to be sure this would be as fine a covered mall as we could make it. I devoted as much of my personal energy to that center and the adjacent Crown Center Hotel as I ever have to any architectural project.

Ed Barnes designed the retailing area, and Harry Weese of Chicago did the hotel. The two men are good friends, worked together well and gave us a superb complex directly across from the offices and fountain.

The tri-level retail center actually bridges Grand Avenue and ties the west side of the neighborhood with the east. There are 400,000 square feet of space in the structure and it contains more than eighty stores. We planned it so it would complement the downtown area and not compete with it directly. Things must have come out pretty well because I am told that our center is now Kansas City's number-one tourist attraction.

Ed Barnes fronted the shops with sixty-foot windows of English glass. Immediately inside is the international cafe and marketplace that was designed for us by Phil George and Irv Harper, a couple of New York boys who had helped us at other times with store interiors and exhibitions.

While the office buildings and the shops got Crown Center off to an exciting and successful beginning, I was especially occupied with the Crown Center Hotel. It was constructed at the same time as the retail center and actually opened earlier. The hotel was of personal interest because both Victor Gruen and, later, Ed Barnes had master planned the hotel for the Signboard Hill location. One of the early recommendations was to level the hill.

It seemed to us that the hill could become a landmark for the entire Crown Center area. When Harry Weese was brought in to design the hotel, he decided the hill would be the focal point of his architecture. He not only retained the hill but used it dramatically as the "back wall" of the rectangular building that houses all of the hotel's public

118

areas. The guest rooms were then contained in an L-shaped tower rising fifteen stories atop the limestone outcrop that had once been such a community eyesore.

The slope of the hill — now inside the lobby building — intrigued me. There was no question to either Donald or me that it should be a garden, with a waterfall. But I also felt that hotel guests and visitors should have the chance to stroll up and down this garden — actually walk through it. We heard about a young man from Arkansas named Bob Shaheen and he executed a plan that has gotten more beautiful each year. His sixty-foot waterfall cascades down the limestone and is surrounded by healthy plants, flowers and trees. But best of all, a winding wooden stairway traverses the hillside from lower right to upper left, bridging the water along the way.

The hotel itself has been a great success. It is managed with careful attention by Western International Hotels, the people we wanted for this important facility.

Today we are building a second hotel, just a block from the Crown Center Hotel. It will be one of the outstanding Hyatt Regency operations, and I have every confidence that Donald and his management team will make it as beautiful and successful as "my" hotel.

After the Crown Center Hotel opened in May, 1973, we turned our attention to two additional Crown Center projects, the first residential community and the second office complex.

For the design of a condominium tower and an apartment complex, we contacted the Cambridge, Massachusetts, firm of The Architects Collaborative, best known by their initials, TAC. Norman Fletcher was the principal we worked with, and he has given us the quality community we desired, one that is attracting residents to Crown Center. There are about 250 homes in all, and the people there can walk undercover to all other sections of Crown Center. In the next decade, an additional two thousand residential units will be added.

In 1975, a joint venture of Mutual Benefit Life Insurance Company, IBM and Walter H. Shorenstein, put up a twenty-eight-story office tower and four-story satellite building in Crown Center. They selected the Chicago architects Fujikawa, Conterato, Lohan and Associates to design this complex, with Bruno Conterato as the principal. Bruno's buildings are a strong, wholly-compatible section of Ed Barnes' master plan.

CROWN CENTER

The Crown Center master plan is kept up to date in a scale model which encompasses the eighty-six acres included in the five hundred million dollar project. Working with the model and overseeing the site are aspects of management which hold great interest for J.C. Hall and Donald Hall.

Aerial view of Hallmark headquarters before development of Crown Center

Crown Center (counterclockwise from Hallmark headquarters): Offices; Crown Center Hotel; condominium tower; the central square surrounded by terraces, retail shops, Halls Crown Center and the American Restaurant

1.

2.

7.

8.

13.

14.

18.

19.

4.

6.

10.

11.

12.

. "Shiva," sculpture by Alexander Calder; 4. Christmas decorations; 5. Crown Center Hotel; 8. American Restaurant; 13. Lobby waterfall, Crown Center Hotel; 14. Crown Center Hotel; 15. International Cafe; 23. International Cafe. All remaining photos depict activities on the Crown Center Square.

16.

17.

21.

22.

23.

Throughout the design of Crown Center, we have worked with gifted and dedicated people. A few that come to mind are Paul Laszlo of Beverly Hills who designed the interior for our Halls Crown Center store; Warren Platner of New Haven who created the award-winning American Restaurant, one of the most beautiful I have ever seen; and, most especially, a large group of Hallmark managers and designers who have made a transition from greeting cards to real estate that none of us thought possible ten years ago.

While Crown Center may have been my dream in the beginning, it has been my son's responsibility from its inception. He spearheaded the drive to expand the concept, and today's Crown Center is beyond anything I had ever visualized in the beginning. It has not been an easy job. The guidelines were not too clear in 1968, since nothing of this magnitude had ever been done before by a private company using private funds. There were two lengthy construction strikes in the late 1960s which set us back more than a year. Then a fire in the early construction stages of the hotel caused concern and a two-month delay.

But for the most part, we have been extremely fortunate. The people of Kansas City and the city fathers have cheered us on.

National writers have called Crown Center a contemporary interpretation of the ancient market places, such as the Greek agora, the Roman bazaars, and the piazzas of the Middle Ages. To me it represents something simpler — a place where people in Kansas City can spend pleasant days and nights experiencing what is new in the arts, food, shopping and just plain good living.

PART III:
SENTIMENTAL ATTACHMENTS

Growing Up Together

During all the years of building the business, my social life was not simply limited, it was almost nonexistent. About the only vacation I'd ever taken was unforgettable for all the wrong reasons. My brothers, Rollie and Bill, convinced me that we should drive to Indianapolis to see the great auto races. The three of us piled into my Hupmobile and set off early on a Friday morning in May, 1915. It was raining and only got worse as we plowed through mud all day. By nightfall we were mired in a mudhole on Mineola Hill in eastern Missouri. The races were to begin the next morning at ten, and we were still about 350 miles from Indianapolis.

At dawn the roads were in even worse condition. We managed to make it only to St. Louis by ten, but to our great relief we learned the races had been rained out and were postponed to Monday. The roads in Illinois were no better, and when a tire blew out, Rollie blew up: "This is a hell of a vacation." By now the car was stuck so deep there was no hope of getting out even if we could change the tire. So we spent Saturday night in the car, too.

Sometime on Sunday we were on our way again. I was the only one who could drive, and it was nonstop from then on. Monday, we arrived in Indianapolis ten minutes before the races began. When they were over, I had a bite to eat and went to bed. I didn't wake up until Tuesday morning.

It was still raining, and we knew the roads would be bad for four or five days. Rollie and Bill had never been to New York, and the roads were paved in that direction almost all the way. When we got in the car,

I said, "Let's go to New York instead." It took us a couple of days. We called on some of our suppliers and looked around the shops for new ideas. We saw a couple of Broadway shows. Then I suggested we go down to Washington, D.C., where none of us had been, and return to Kansas City from there.

The capital was a wonderful and welcome sight. I'm sorry that today Washington isn't the way it was back then, when it still looked as if it had been laid out to fit its population. We did everything first-time visitors do, but it was a small incident that remains in my memory. We decided to have a real treat for lunch by going to a fine restaurant. I had an appetite that was big enough for all three of us. But I was shortly to lose it. About halfway through my soup course, which seemed delicious, I found myself staring at the bottom of the bowl — there, lying flat on its back, was a huge cockroach that had shared my soup with unfavorable results.

Though this trip certainly was troublesome, it provided us with many good stories to tell back home. And we took advantage of any chance to cheer up my mother. She had been ill and unable to get around many years of her life. It had been four years since she came to Kansas City and a new life. She remained interested in everything we did — and in our hopeful future. Our business was simple then, and I wish she could have lived long enough to see it develop. At least she did see her family raised, as she had vowed she would, and for a few years of her life she was not wanting for anything we could give her.

By 1916 our brave little mother developed a malignancy. We took her to the Mayo Clinic in Rochester for surgery. There was little hope. She died at the age of fifty-six. Many years later my brothers and I were able to honor her memory in an appropriate way. We established the Nancy Dudley Hall Laboratory of Mammalian Genetics at the University of Kansas. It is a four-story building dedicated to the research and study of genetics. In spite of my mother's many illnesses, her life was all giving — and now through the memorial laboratory, it always will be.

Two events changed my life for the better — meeting a lovely young lady named Elizabeth Ann Dilday and buying a Stutz automobile, which

I had always fancied but never thought I could afford.

I had driven my Hupmobile over one hundred thousand miles since 1913; then for about six months I had an Auburn. That was the shortest life of any car I have ever owned. Most of the paint had peeled off in that time, and the dealer refused to do anything about it. It wasn't hard to understand why he soon went out of business.

The Stutz wasn't new. That would have cost about two thousand dollars, which I could never have afforded. But it was a great bargain at six hundred dollars. (A new Ford at the time cost around three hundred dollars.) The man who sold it was in a financial squeeze. The Stutz had completely vamped me. It was an olive-green touring car (meaning it carried four passengers) with tan seats of heavy cowhide that never showed any wear. It had a convertible top and accordion curtains.

The car was as strong as an ox with fenders so thick they could tear the wooden slats off a streetcar. And that's exactly what happened one day when a motorman misjudged the width of a narrow street and ripped past me. I just brushed the wooden slivers off the fender with my auto gloves, and there was no damage to the car. Everybody had respect for a Stutz. It was by far the greatest automobile I have ever owned, and I kept it longer than any other car.

My sister, Marie, introduced me to her schoolmate Elizabeth Ann Dilday. Actually, Marie was going to visit Elizabeth's two-year-old niece, Lucy Jean, who was a real charmer. It was a case of love at first sight for me — with the niece, that is. We all went for a ride in my Stutz.

After that I occasionally found an evening or Sunday afternoon to spare from business to take Lucy Jean and Elizabeth for a ride. And before I knew it I was taking Elizabeth for rides even after Lucy Jean had gone back to her home in Arkansas. Soon after she left, Elizabeth was told that Lucy Jean was quite ill, and she went to Arkansas to be with her. It wasn't long before Elizabeth notified me that the child had passed away. She asked me to give the sad news to her mother, Lucy Jean's grandmother. This was about the toughest assignment I have ever had. Elizabeth stayed with her sister for a time, then came back to Kansas City. Sharing the loss of the little girl brought us closer together.

Elizabeth and I enjoyed many of the same things — the theater, horseback riding and automobile trips without the traffic hassle of today. In fact, I suspected then that the thing Elizabeth really liked about me was my car. But we were together for fifty-five years, with three children, eleven grandchildren and even great-grandchildren.

After we married we settled down in Kansas City with the promise that when summer came we would go on a honeymoon in the Stutz. By then I found out that I hadn't known the whole story about the car. The motor needed a complete overhaul, and it was necessary in those days to have it done at the factory in Indianapolis, where Elizabeth lived before coming to Kansas City. We decided to drive there first, then go on to Quebec for our honeymoon.

We arrived in Indianapolis and delivered the car to the service manager of the factory. He said it would take ten days to overhaul the motor. That was all the time we had allotted for the entire trip. I asked if something temporary couldn't be done about the car leaking oil like a sieve so we could still take our trip. His solution was to use tractor oil and leave the car in Indianapolis on our way back from Quebec.

About every one hundred miles we had to put in a quart or two of tractor oil that was as heavy as molasses. We bought it in gallon cans, and when we'd run out we could only hope we'd soon get to another big town. We encountered other crises on the road that had nothing to do with the oil supply. The automobile was capable of doing seventy or eighty miles an hour, but it had no shock absorbers, just heavy springs. It was hard to find a road smooth enough to drive more than forty miles an hour.

One day in the western part of New York, we were on a rough gravel road, and I was bouncing up and down when a wasp, with excellent timing, slipped directly under me. When I came down on the thing, I thought I had been shot. I immediately pulled off the road. We picked up a cushion at a variety store and kept right on traveling, but for the next couple of days I almost wished I *had* been shot instead of stung.

On the trip back I got stung again — but in an entirely different way. A filling station attendant warned us that a small town ahead had set up a "speed trap." I drove with extreme care as we approached the town with both of us watching the speedometer. We were stopped all the same. The constable just assumed that a Stutz would be going too fast. For about two hours we talked with the judge in a little police court he had set up in his home. Nothing we said had any effect on him. Finally, I told him I wasn't going to pay any fine since I was in the right. The judge

132

accused me of contempt of court and threatened to lock me up. I asked to use the phone and called an attorney in Kansas City to come to our rescue. The judge didn't like the idea of the publicity that might result if an attorney came that far to take the case. He backed down, and we paid no fine at all.

Our first child was born on July 8, 1922. We named her Elizabeth Ann, after her mother. A year and a half later our second daughter, Barbara Louise, arrived on October 21. Our only son was born July 9, 1928. The family was unanimous for naming him Joyce. But I had fought the battle of having a girl's name all my life, and I did not want to wish it on my son. We compromised, naming him Donald Joyce.

In 1927 a friend told us about a house on forty-one acres with wonderful trees and a stream running through the property. It was just over the Missouri line in Kansas and was then considered well out in the country. In a few days we were owners of a home in the country. The property had a fine little horse barn as well as excellent pasture and woodland for riding. My wife was fond of riding horses and taught me to enjoy the sport.

My mother-in-law was living with us, and she was great company for Elizabeth since I was traveling so much. Rollie spent most of his weekends at our place as well. After the birth of our son, we began to feel a little crowded for space. We decided to add on to the house, but after working several months on plans, we realized the rooms were just too small. We would plunge right in and build a new house on the same site, moving the old house to another part of the property.

We were outside the limits of any fire protection; so we planned the house to be as fireproof as possible. It would be Georgian style, built of concrete and steel with a stone and brick exterior. It was completed in 1930, and today is on a little more than six hundred acres. The city has since moved out and around the property, but the house is far enough back in the woods to still enjoy the quiet country atmosphere.

Summers in Kansas City can be unbearably hot and humid, and it wasn't long before we felt the need for a vacation house near water where it would be cool. Colorado was our choice. After checking with a number of realtors with no results, I put an ad in the *Denver Post*. A man sent a photograph of a Swiss chalet-style house built on a rocky

Elizabeth Ann Dilday

Elizabeth Ann Dilday Hall with Stutz Bearcat in 1921

Joyce and Elizabeth Hall with Elizabeth Ann and Barbara in 1923

Elizabeth Hall with Elizabeth Ann, Barbara and Donald around 1931

Joyce Hall

J.C. Hall with Del Masco

Elizabeth Hall and Barbara

Joyce Hall with children at Grand Lake

136

Joyce Hall with Rollie B. Hall at Grand Lake

Grand Lake lodge

Donald, about eight years old

bluff overlooking Grand Lake. We planned to rent it for two weeks but liked it so much we stayed seven. We continued to rent it for seven summers, then bought it.

Important mail and artwork would arrive each day. And occasionally my secretary would come for short stays. This way I was able to take more extended vacations and still conduct business. Rollie would visit us frequently. He introduced me to trout fishing in a mountain stream that ran down to the lake from an altitude of about eleven thousand feet. I soon learned that to find anything more exciting than trout fishing in a mountain stream would be a hard assignment.

We fished together for about twenty-five summers, until Rollie was no longer able to take the punishment of climbing over the rocks. I had always been fond of Rollie, but these daily trips up the east fork of the Colorado River gave us an understanding and closeness that I doubt we could have achieved any other way.

On one excursion in late September we stayed out too late and got lost trying to get back to the trail. It was going to be a cold night. We have always owned a German shepherd, and one of the most remarkable was named Del Masco. He was with us that evening. The only thing I could think of was to get Masco to lead us home. We tied a fish line to his collar and kept shouting, "Go home, Masco. Go home." In about an hour we were back at the house sitting down to a warm dinner.

Masco loved our country property in Kansas City, too. He was in his glory, with ten acres fenced in — and plenty of squirrels and rabbits to chase. He never could catch them but never stopped trying.

We also had a Jersey cow to give us fresh milk. She was from the famous Longview herd and was with calf when we bought her. We were hoping she'd produce a heifer, but instead we got a bull and didn't know quite what to do with him. But a man who worked for us named Johnson said he could handle him.

By the time the bull was two years old, he was nothing to toy with. One Sunday I looked out at the fenced-in barn lot and saw Johnson with a pitchfork holding off the charging bull. Johnson was a big man, over six feet tall and strong, but the bull knocked him down, breaking the handle of the fork in half. I ran out thinking I could attract the bull's attention. By now the bull had rammed Johnson a couple of hard blows with his horns, and Johnson was almost unconscious. I picked up the fork half and hit the bull square in the face. That stopped him for a moment, but he was soon attacking Johnson again.

I called Masco, who came running. Just as the bull started for me, Masco jumped on the gate and knocked it open. He seized a back leg of the bull in his jaws and was biting at the tendon. That allowed me to get to Johnson. Masco kept circling the bull while I dragged Johnson out. I called Masco, who came immediately, and I closed the gate.

Masco was not a vicious dog, but he would protect any of us to the death — me, the children and especially Elizabeth, who fed him. Coming back from a mountain trip after dark, with Masco always walking right in front of Elizabeth, we heard a rustle in the brush. The next thing we knew, Masco attacked a porcupine, thinking he was protecting Elizabeth. By the time we could call him off, he was shot full of quills. We worked all night pulling them out, then went to Estes Park the next morning to have a doctor treat him. He died on the examining table.

The family and the business really grew up together. At the time the children were born, the business was small but profitable — and growing rapidly. It had always been such a fascinating business that it commanded all my time. It was my work and my hobby. I put in long hours at the office six days a week and carried a full briefcase home every night.

Often I'd bring artwork home to examine for improvement and ideas. From the time the children were old enough to toddle, they loved to see the pictures. And no one was more interested than their mother. Elizabeth was becoming quite an expert on greeting cards. Because of this, I guess, she put up with the evenings and weekends I worked in those early years. When our girls, Elizabeth and Barbara, reached school age, they too were having ideas about greeting cards.

By then the company had distribution in every state, and I was anxious to know what went on in the field. The car would be shipped to some area of the country, and the whole family would pile on the train. (In those days a car could be shipped by train for little more than the passenger fare.) We always selected an area that was of the greatest interest to the family and one that was new to me. We'd spend ten days driving around the territory.

Often when I visited a store, I'd buy a greeting card and engage the dealer in a conversation about business without ever indicating who I was. Occasionally I'd introduce myself and candidly discuss problems with him. These trips gave me an understanding of the territories and the difficulties salesmen and dealers faced.

My son, Donald, was introduced to the greeting card business as soon as he was aware of what it was. From the time he was born, I was hopeful he would come into the business and even succeed me. But I didn't want to encourage him unless he was sure it was what he wanted. To the best of a proud father's ability, I did nothing to influence him in his decision. He became a sales trainee for us in 1946 and worked as a sales representative on weekends while attending Dartmouth College. After completing school and a tour of duty in the army, he joined the company as assistant to the president in 1953. By this time he knew a lot more about the business than I did when I started it.

His first years with the company could not have been easy for him. Being the boss's son is never easy. He is judged more critically than others — not only by the people he works with but by the boss himself. A mistake that might go unnoticed if made by someone else becomes a matter of consequence if made by the boss's son. While I am conscious of the prejudice of a father, I am also a critical and inquisitive person, and I believe I would have known if any problems had been created — and I never heard of any.

Now, in 1978, Donald has had twelve years as president of the company, while I have served as chairman of the board. It has been one of the greatest satisfactions of my life to see the remarkable success he has enjoyed.

During the height of the Depression, I began to feel that the only thing I could depend on was real estate. I started to put everything I could into land as early as 1930. I bought parcels of ground adjoining our farm, until a few years after the Depression we had accumulated seven hundred acres. We had kept a few cows and horses on the forty acres we started with. Now it was apparent we were going to have to do some real farming.

In 1935 I learned that a fine herd of Jersey cattle was to be auctioned off by the estate of a wealthy lumberman, R. A. Long. I had always liked Jerseys and thought that raising them would stimulate my interest in farming — which needed stimulating. We bought thirty-eight head of the most promising animals in the sale. Then we built a model barn to house this prize herd. It created a great deal of interest in the dairy industry.

There were a few things I hadn't taken into consideration in owning a Jersey herd. The most important was that it took a lot of time, and I was already in a business that took more than full time. I also thought it would be enjoyable to show fine Jerseys and try to win blue ribbons! but I soon found out this wasn't my kind of fun. In showing against a farmer who had put his heart into raising one exceptional animal, I felt sorry if I won — but I felt sorry if I lost, too.

And something that shouldn't have come as a surprise — I was in the dairy business. Cows keep up their milk production only if they are milked twice a day at exactly the same time. This means if they are milked at 4:00 p.m., they have to be milked at 4:00 a.m. as well.

Jersey milk had sold at a premium because it had the highest percentage of butterfat, but American women were just beginning to get serious about dieting. Before we knew it, we had surplus milk. We decided to send it down to the plant and give everybody a glass to renew their energies. I'm not sure it increased production, but it created goodwill among our people — and some problems. Our employees were also concerned about drinking rich milk. So we gave them an additional choice of iced tea in the summer and coffee in the winter. We've been told that this practice started the "coffee break" in American industry. However, we make no official claim to originating this dubious custom.

We continued to fight the battle of selling rich milk, with the public increasingly wanting thinner milk. The final blow came when the man who managed our herd developed an allergy to cattle — and left. After that I decided there must be an easier way to lose money and sold the herd.

While I was trying to decide what to do with an empty dairy barn, I got a call from John Rockefeller Prentice, who was a grandson of John D. Rockefeller. He was developing an artificial insemination program to improve dairy herds and had read about our barn. He said he would like a ten-year lease, and we came to an agreement.

In the next few months, Prentice spent about forty thousand dollars putting the barn in shape for his operation. He rented the pastureland

Georgian house built by Hall family in 1930

Dairy barn

Joyce Hall at the farm

A family birthday gathering

Joyce and Elizabeth Hall

from us as well. By early fall he was ready for business. A few weeks later fresh hay had been put in the mow in the afternoon. It had been a warm day, and the hay was still damp. As a result, spontaneous combustion occurred that night, and within minutes the barn was in flames.

Many fine bulls were on the lower floor, and there was just time to turn them out. It all happened so fast the bulls couldn't be driven into corrals and were running wild. Crowds came from all directions to watch the fire. Somehow the bulls were finally led into corrals, and miraculously no one was injured — although one car was almost destroyed when a bull charged it.

Over the years I learned a number of ways to lose money in farming. But I never expected to have to report this to the leading businessmen in our community. While I was still quite young, with a small but fairly successful business, I met an important investment banker in town, H. P. Wright. Among other things, he was involved in organizing and financing Sinclair Oil. He had gone out of his way to be friendly to me, and I greatly admired him.

He invited me to be a guest at his study club, where thirty distinguished men met monthly for an evening of discussion. Without realizing what I was getting into, I felt his invitation had to be accepted. I was almost frightened to find myself seated next to the chairman, Paul Patton, a man with a great reputation as a contractor. He was known to take on the most complex projects and to do them better, faster and cheaper than anyone else. It also fascinated me that Patton had bought Buffalo Bill's ranch in Montana.

After dinner Patton read a rather formal paper on wheat. It applied particularly to government subsidies, even dating back to the Egyptians. Patton made the most complicated statistics interesting, and I soon found myself completely relaxed.

For the rest of the evening each man around the table added anything he could to the subject. They were all of similar standing — a judge, a university president, a banker and two of the most impressive men I have known in my life, Henry J. Haskell, the chief editorial writer of the *Kansas City Star*, and Roy Roberts, the managing editor. It was apparent they had all given the subject of wheat serious consideration.

144

And I was getting increasingly uncomfortable trying to think of what I would say. The few things that occurred to me had been said by someone else.

When my turn came, I explained that I'd never given much thought to wheat. I was raised in corn and cattle country, but I knew little about farming in general. Then it occurred to me that I could prove it. I told them about a farmer on the property adjoining ours. He had proposed that we each feed half a carload of cattle for one summer and sell them in the fall.

About the middle of August he called to tell me that cattle prices were good and the pastures were getting dry, making it a good time to sell. After selling both herds, he said he couldn't understand what had happened to my cattle. My grass was as good as his, and the stream dividing our pastures provided plenty of water. All the same his cattle had put on considerable weight during the summer and mine had lost. While he made about four hundred dollars on the transaction, I lost an equal amount. This was at a time when four hundred dollars was more like four thousand dollars.

The only difference he could see was that I had shade trees in my pasture, and on hot afternoons my cattle would lie around while his would be eating grass. To me it was just a matter of one man knowing what he was doing and the other being a greenhorn. This didn't vary much from what I had observed about farmers when I was a boy. Two brothers could inherit equal sections of land, and year after year one would be able to pay his bills and have a bank balance and the other would buy on credit and have a bank loan. But the unsuccessful one would still continue to run his farm.

The difference I saw between farming and any other occupation was that if a man started a newspaper, for instance, and wasn't a good operator, he would go broke. But a poor farmer carries on; there is no elimination of the inefficient operator. And I assumed it had probably always been that way with farming. As a result, government subsidies became necessary. Mine was the shortest statement of the evening, but I got some applause — probably because I was a guest.

Good Neighbors, Great Presidents

Roy Roberts later became president of the *Kansas City Star* and one of my closest friends. He advised me wisely on any really tough problems I had. During his time, Roy met all the greats in our country and many others as well. He was interested in everything, especially politics, and he had the respect of the leaders of both parties.

It was through Roy and U.S. Senator Harry Darby of Kansas that I first met General Dwight D. Eisenhower early in 1950. The general, then head of NATO, had given his home town of Abilene, Kansas, permission to build a museum to house his war trophies. After the death of his mother in 1946, the five Eisenhower brothers donated their boyhood home to the city, and the museum was to be built on the same grounds. I was asked to serve on the museum committee.

Before the museum was started, the general agreed to run for the Republican nomination for president in 1952. He decided to announce his candidacy in Abilene, and a groundbreaking ceremony for the museum was arranged at the same time. We were all charmed by his down-to-earth manner.

After his election, we began making the personal and official Christmas cards for United States presidents. Being an artist himself, Eisenhower was most challenging and imaginative to deal with. We felt strongly that he should use his own paintings on the cards, but he didn't think they were good enough. He had recently done a portrait of Abraham Lincoln which we thought was an excellent choice — a portrait of one president painted by another.

President Eisenhower loved to fish at St. Louis Creek in Colorado, about twenty miles from our place at Grand Lake. On a trip there in September, 1955, he had his first heart attack. He hadn't quite finished a painting of the creek when he was rushed to Fitzsimmons Hospital in Denver. The painting was to be his Christmas card that year, and he asked me to visit him to discuss it since he wasn't sure he could finish it in time. When I got to the hospital he had already started working on it again. Can anyone doubt what great therapy painting was for him?

President Eisenhower originated the People to People program early in his first term. It was defined as "a voluntary, nationwide effort by private citizens of the United States to work for peace through the development of mutual respect, friendship and understanding with people of other countries." He asked me to be chairman of the executive committee.

After Eisenhower left office in 1961, the program was just getting under way when I was asked to help plan the rededication of Liberty Memorial in Kansas City. The 217-foot monument, honoring those who had died in World War I, had been dedicated forty years before by Vice President Calvin Coolidge. The rededication to peace related perfectly to the People to People slogan: "Working for peace through understanding." We would need General Eisenhower's approval to involve People to People, and I hoped he'd make the principal address. He liked the idea and accepted. I gave the news to the press.

Shortly thereafter I learned that former President Harry S. Truman had also been asked to make an address. There was great concern that neither man would attend after hearing the other had accepted. It had been more than eight years since the two had spoken to each other — at President Eisenhower's inauguration in 1953. Although both had attended President Kennedy's inauguration, they didn't exchange a word. This put me in an embarrassing position. We could hardly withdraw the invitation to either of these men.

I was not aware of what had prompted the rift between them and thought this event might bring about a reconciliation. But everyone I discussed it with said the trouble couldn't be patched up. A ceremony dedicated to world understanding wouldn't look very good if two of the country's former presidents didn't even have a personal understanding. *Newsweek* magazine reported: "It's people-to-people for everybody — except Ike and Harry."

Arthur Mag, an attorney and friend of Truman's, got us an appointment with the president at the Truman Library in Independence, Missouri. It was difficult to tell Mr. Truman the entire story without ever using General Eisenhower's name. But I thought if I did, he'd throw me out. He listened attentively, and I kept right on talking to keep him from saying no. After about thirty minutes, there just wasn't anything more to say.

President Truman smiled and said, "You've probably heard that Ike and I don't always see eye to eye." I admitted there was a rumor to that effect. Then he said, "But this is different. I like his People to People program, and I'll do anything I can to help solve your problem. Just tell Ike that if he'll come to Kansas City for the ceremony and stop by the library here, I'll meet him on the bottom step with both arms extended."

The next day I went to Gettysburg to see General Eisenhower. Somehow I thought it would be easier to get his approval — it wasn't. But finally the general reluctantly agreed to attend the rededication as well as visit the Truman Library.

There were problems right up to the day of the ceremony, November 11, 1961. It was an off-year election, and the two ex-presidents were especially interested in a senatorial contest in Texas and one for governor in New Jersey. President Truman, in his familiar style, blasted the men Eisenhower supported. As a result, the general called me to cancel his appearance at the ceremony. I tried to change his mind, but he said he would only agree to attend the People to People board meeting to be held the same day.

Then only a week before the ceremony, President Truman, in jest, commented to the press: "Mr. Hoover and I have formed a Former President's Club. He's president and I'm secretary. The other fellow hasn't been taken in yet." This riled the general, too.

Senator Darby, Roy Roberts and I met the general's plane. He was polite as always but seemed a little ruffled when he got in the car. We headed for the Truman Library without really knowing whether he was willing to go until we were about halfway there. And, of course, we hadn't dared send word to President Truman that we were on our way. Then General Eisenhower asked that the motorcycle escort turn off its sirens. As we were approaching the library, President Truman had no warning at all that we were almost there. But as we arrived, Truman came bounding down the steps buttoning his suit coat. Just as the general emerged from the car, the president reached the bottom step with both arms extended as he had promised.

General Eisenhower was smiling faintly as President Truman greeted him: "I'm glad to see you. Come in, come in." The two went into the president's office to talk privately. About a half hour later, they came out smiling broadly. General Eisenhower asked if he should sign the guest register, and Mr. Truman replied, "Definitely, then if anything is missing, we'll know who to blame." They stopped in front of a portrait of the general, and Truman asked jovially, "You know who that fellow is, don't you?" Mr. Truman escorted him to an exact replica of the oval office. Then Truman excused himself saying, "I don't want to go any farther. There's too much of me in there."

That evening General and Mrs. Eisenhower and President and Mrs. Truman joined us for cocktails. They had enjoyed the rededication ceremony and were spirited and friendly. I was pleased that they met on several other occasions after that, finally ending an eight-year period of animosity.

It wasn't until some time later that I learned how the Eisenhower-Truman feud came about. Anna Rosenberg, who had been Truman's assistant secretary of defense, congratulated me on bringing the two presidents together. Then she explained that before General Eisenhower's inauguration, President Truman asked her, "Anna, if you were about to become president of the United States and you had a son in the army, where would you want him on Inauguration Day — in Korea or Washington?" She replied, "In Washington, of course."

Mr. Truman then instructed her to issue an order for Colonel John Eisenhower to report to Washington. General Eisenhower was furious that he hadn't been consulted. Speculation was that he also suspected the president's motive was to undercut his son since Eisenhower felt John had his best assignment in the army to date. In the military world, this was not an illogical interpretation — however, Anna Rosenberg told me that that had never occurred to Mr. Truman.

General Eisenhower showed his resentment first by declining to attend a briefing at the White House, which didn't set well with Mr. Truman. On Inauguration Day, the general further rebuffed Truman when he arrived at the White House to pick up the outgoing president. Protocol called for the general to escort the president to the car — instead he simply sent word that he was waiting. President Truman had a fine-honed temper himself, and the two men scarcely spoke that day — and not at all for eight more years until the two ex-presidents met at the steps of the Truman Library.

Even though we had been members of the same general community

Season's Greetings
1958

Official card sent by President and Mrs. Dwight D. Eisenhower, Christmas, 1958

THE PRESIDENT'S HOUSE, WASHINGTON.

Official card sent by President and Mrs. Gerald R. Ford, 1974

WE WANTED TO PUT SOMETHING OF OURSELVES IN OUR CHRISTMAS CARD TO YOU....

Personal Christmas card sent by Presiden[t] and Mrs. Eisenhower in 195[ ]

Card reproduced in 1963 for the benefit of the National Cultural Center from an original painting by Jacqueline Kennedy

Six consecutive United States Presidents have had their Christmas Cards designed by Hallmark. President Eisenhower was the first. He and Mrs. Eisenhower were the only first family sending both official and personal greetings. The Eisenhowers sent about 1,300 cards. Succeeding presidents, like many other Americans, apparently had trouble limiting their Christmas card list. The Kennedy's sent 2,300 cards. The Carters sent 60,000 cards in 1977.

Official card sent by President and Mrs. Jimmy Carter, Christmas, 1977

P

PEOPLE
to
PEOPLE

In 1956, President Dwight D. Eisenhower invited a nucleus of well-known business leaders (including Joyce Hall) to a White House conference to establish an organization composed of citizens dedicated to the pursuit of world peace. People to People, the organization that evolved from this meeting, is a non-political, non-profit organization working outside of government to attain this goal.

At left and facing page, Joyce C. Hall with former president Dwight D. Eisenhower at rededication of the Liberty Memorial in Kansas City in 1961

Mamie Eisenhower presenting Eisenhower Medallion to Joyce C. Hall recognizing his contribution to world peace through his work with the People to People program

Hall and former president Eisenhower looking over a map on a 1962 train trip through the St. Lo valley in France

for many years, I didn't see much of Harry S. Truman before he became a United States senator. He lived in Independence, Missouri, and I lived in Johnson County, Kansas, about twenty-five miles apart. Also, I was a Kansas Republican, and he was a Missouri Democrat.

As a senator, Truman had done an outstanding job as chairman of the Senate Committee to Investigate the National Defense Program. In fact, it was his work on what became known as the Truman Committee that led to his selection as President Franklin D. Roosevelt's running mate in 1944.

Still, when President Roosevelt died in April, 1945, I didn't know what to expect from Mr. Truman. I was impressed by his humble approach to the presidency and found little to criticize in his performance. But when he came up for election in 1948, almost everyone felt he just wasn't going to make it.

A few days before the election, President Truman arrived in Kansas City from his whistle-stop tour to relax and play cards with friends. He was certain he was going to be elected — and he meant it. Most of us thought the president's confidence was naive to say the least — and now we all know who was naive.

President Truman was frank and fearless. I thought what a good thing it would be if everyone in public life was as honest and decisive. He had a routine in arriving at decisions. Once presented with a problem, he would ask for proposals in writing from his key people. He would study them carefully and mark points he wanted to consider. Then he'd think about them into the night, go promptly to sleep and have his decision the following day.

My admiration for President Truman grew as we worked together on several projects. He was always loyal to his friends, even when he was criticized for it. And his friends returned that loyalty. President Truman's birthday became a celebrated tradition in Kansas City. His local friends attend as well as friends from all over the world.

To me the finest tribute to President Truman's record in office was paid by Sir Winston Churchill in 1962, when he addressed the president directly in a speech: "You, more than any other man, have saved Western civilization. When the British could no longer hold out in Greece, you, and you alone, sir, made the decision that saved that ancient land from the Communists. You acted in a similar fashion...when the Soviets tried to take over Iran. Then there was your

154

resolute stand on Trieste, and your Marshall Plan which rescued Western Europe.... Then you established the North Atlantic Treaty Alliance and collective security for those nations against the military machinations of the Soviet Union. Then there was your audacious Berlin Airlift. And, of course, there was Korea."

Could anything more be said to honor any president?

In July, 1962, General Eisenhower was asked to address the World Confederation of Organizations of the Teaching Profession at its annual convention in Stockholm, Sweden. The general and I felt that this was an excellent association for People to People, and we made plans to sail on the *Queen Elizabeth*. Our party included the Eisenhowers and their grandchildren, David, then fourteen years old and Barbara Ann, then thirteen; Mr. and Mrs. Freeman Gosden and their fourteen-year-old son Craig; my granddaughter Libby Marshall, who was about to turn twelve; and myself. The Gosdens were old and dear friends of the Eisenhowers. Freeman had played Amos on the "Amos and Andy" radio show, one of the most popular programs of all time.

The second day out was Libby's birthday, one she'll never forget. Mrs. Eisenhower had the chef create an enormous English fruitcake with a thick marzipan frosting. It was big enough for everybody in the dining room to have a piece. When Libby gave General Eisenhower his cake, she got a big hug and kiss in return.

On the morning of July 23 we docked at Cherbourg, France. From there we went by train to Paris where the general was to see President Charles de Gaulle. The French had provided a private train that was so new the electricians were still installing lights when we boarded. The general invited Libby and me to sit in the observation car, which afforded a panoramic view of the countryside.

Without expecting it, we were to travel the river valley route of the Normandy invasion with General Eisenhower reliving it for us. This was the first time he had been back. The train had only been under way a few minutes when the general asked if I had noticed the name of the town we had just passed — St. Lo. Eighteen years before, on D-Day — after establishing a beachhead — St. Lo was the breakthrough that insured the successful invasion.

His enthusiasm was contagious as he continued to reminisce. He wanted a map, and Libby remembered she had one in her bag. The general began tracing the trip down the valley. He pointed out a small culvert under a gravel road and said, "There was one of the most dangerous positions I was in during my soldiering." He explained that just as he had come down the hill and crossed the culvert in an open jeep, the Germans back in the woods began shooting. His group had no cover and ducked down in the jeep. The driver steered by peeking out the lower corner of the windshield.

As the train moved up a valley to the north, General Eisenhower said it was here that they could see Field Marshal Viscount Montgomery's troops heading toward them, surrounding the Germans. After three days of heavy fighting, he said there were so many bodies of German soldiers there was hardly a place to walk.

We arrived in Paris, and the Eisenhowers visited President de Gaulle, then went on to Bonn, West Germany, to see Chancellor Konrad Adenhauer. We caught up with them again in Copenhagen, a favorite city of mine with a favorite hotel, the Angleterre. That night the general took us to Tivoli, one of the greatest entertainment parks in the world. But it was difficult to see much because General Eisenhower was constantly surrounded by crowds.

Libby was to meet still another president on this trip. On returning to New York we had lunch with Bill Nichols, then editor and publisher of *This Week* magazine. Bill had an appointment that evening with President Herbert Hoover at the Waldorf Towers, and he arranged for us to go along. Mr. Hoover looked quite feeble, but his mind was sharp and he was cheerful.

It was only a few days after President Hoover's eighty-eighth birthday — and his secretary brought out a huge cardboard box full of birthday greetings. There must have been about three thousand cards, most of them from children the world over. I said that I thought it was wonderful that President Hoover would still be remembered so affectionately. We were all stunned when she told us, "The president answers each one himself." Over the years, he had maintained a correspondence with children here and around the world.

More Than a Sunday Painter

Of the many notable artists we have used on Hallmark cards over the years, there are four who are especially memorable for what their talent and friendship have meant to me — Walt Disney, Grandma Moses, Norman Rockwell and Winston S. Churchill.

Walt Disney had lived in Kansas City from about 1910 to 1923. From the time he was a child he was always busy sketching. Disney was still quite young when he was able to open his first studio — in a garage where he had little more than desk space. Writing about this period in his life, Diane Disney Miller, Walt's daughter, quoted him as saying: "Mice gathered in my wastebasket when I worked late at night. I lifted them out and kept them in little cages on my desk. One of them was a particular friend. Then before I left Kansas City, I carefully carried him out into a field and let him go." Can you guess who he grew up to be?

Walt took a job as a cartoonist with the Kansas City Film Ad Company in 1920. He did animations for theater advertisements and became interested in animating his own creations, developing techniques to improve the process. He soon saw a place for himself in the booming movie industry and set off for California in 1923.

He went after any job as long as it was in motion pictures, but Hollywood had no place for him. He continued working on his own and in 1924 produced his first short feature, *Alice in Cartoonland*. He did several more, but it wasn't until 1928 that Walt's all-time favorite character, Mickey Mouse, made his first appearance. Then Walt began dreaming of more ambitious animated features. Our paths did not cross until 1932 — the same year he released *Three Little Pigs*.

His older brother, Roy, came to see us about using Walt's characters on greeting cards. We were charmed by the cartoons and agreed on a contract — the first one made to use Disney characters. They were an outstanding success. From then on, I would visit Walt's studio looking for new ways to use his characters, including Mickey Mouse, Donald Duck, and Pluto — and from his full-length features, *Bambi* and *Snow*

WALT DISNEY

The late Walt Disney began a fine association with Hallmark when his characters first appeared on greeting cards in 1932

158

To Joyes Hall
my Respect &
Admiration
Walt Disney

The work of the late Norman Rockwell, another long-time friend and associate, was used on Hallmark cards for many years

Norman Rockwell

Through the years, Hallmark has recognized the importance of giving their artists the stimulation of exposure to outside artists and experts. In the early fifties, Norman Rockwell was a guest on a number of occasions and shared some of his experiences informally with the group. An artist who was present at these sessions recalls Rockwell's unpretentiousness, his total enjoyment of his association with Hallmark and his many humorous anecdotes.

Grandma Moses at work, — as drawn by norman rockwell july 1949

A Rockwell sketch of a beloved Hallmark contributor, Grandma Moses

Grandma Moses' painting used on a Christmas card

White and the Seven Dwarfs. To this day, his creations appear on our cards and other products.

Walt became a good friend and expert counselor. When Donald and I were considering the development of Crown Center, a commercial and residential complex adjoining our headquarters, I sought the advice of Walt Disney and James Rouse of Baltimore, the builder of model shopping centers. On one of his visits to Kansas City, Jim had just come from Disneyland. He was so intrigued with Disney's operation that he asked if I could get him an appointment with Walt. I had no idea what he wanted to discuss, and I told him that I thought Walt would want to know. A little reluctantly Jim said he wanted to talk about building a city. That struck me as a rather fantastic notion, and I doubted that Walt would have any interest in it.

Sometime later I was visiting Walt in Burbank and asked him about meeting Jim. As I expected, he asked what Jim had in mind. I felt a little foolish saying, "Building a city." But Walt thought big, and without hesitation replied, "Why not?" He laughed and said he had always thought it would be fun to build a city. I called Jim, and he enthusiastically agreed to meet Walt at a beach house we had recently built in Malibu, California.

Donald joined us, and we talked almost the entire day. It became apparent that Walt was working on something important that he was keeping confidential. Finally he told us about it. He was preparing a large General Motors exhibit for the New York World's Fair. He called it a "people mover" — a method of running automobiles over a given route with automated controls in the hands of one man. (I sometimes think that if Walt Disney had lived another ten years, he might have solved the urban transportation problem in America.)

Walt was fascinated by Jim's plans to build a city — although it sounded like quite a dream to me. However, it was eventually realized — and Columbia, Maryland, between Washington, D.C., and Baltimore, exists today because of that dream. While Walt didn't say he had anything else on his mind, it later became clear that he did. Walt was then developing plans for Disney World and EPCOT in Florida. And at the same time, we were working on ideas for our property. While I had not thought of our project as a city, it has since been described as a "city within a city" many times. And I believe it was enlarged and improved because of the creative thinking of these two master builders.

Looking back on that Sunday in Malibu almost twenty years ago, it strikes me as extraordinary that four men, each in his own way yearning to build a city, ultimately did exactly that.

Over the years I saw Walt Disney change from one of the poorest financial risks in the country to one of the safest. He probably received a record number of awards and honors, but always remained a modest man. Everything he did appealed to children and adults alike. He was fully aware of just how bright today's children are. And I wonder if any man was ever known and loved by more people.

I don't think I can express my feelings about Walt Disney better than three little girls did several years before he died. I was flying back from London, seated near three sisters ranging in age from six to twelve. I asked if they'd had a good time in London, and one said, "Yes, but we would rather have gone to California." Surprised, I wondered why. The oldest girl answered, "To see Disneyland and go to Burbank." And what did they want to see in Burbank? She said, "Walt Disney." She knew his studio was there. I asked if they thought Walt Disney was a real man or someone more like Santa Claus. The oldest girl thought this over carefully and answered, "Both." And I agreed with her.

I n the late 1940s probably the two best-loved artists in America — Grandma (Anna Mary Robertson) Moses and Norman Rockwell — began to apply their genius for us. Grandma Moses' primitive style was enchanting — and it was no fluke publicized only because she started painting at the age of seventy. She had great ability as an artist and was equally marvelous as a person.

I visited Grandma Moses several times at her home in upstate New York. On one occasion I casually mentioned a sales convention that we were holding in New York City. She wanted to know how many salesmen would be there — "A lot of them," I said. "But how many?" she asked. I told her about ninety. She said she'd like to attend and give "a little talk to them." Senility was not one of her problems — she was interested in sales.

Norman Rockwell joined us about a year after Grandma Moses. Since they lived a short distance apart, I suggested to Norman that he visit her on her eighty-eighth birthday, September 7, 1948. He did — and made a remarkable sketch of Grandma Moses sitting at her drawing board with a coffeepot on the floor. It was published in the *Saturday Evening Post*. Grandma Moses was upset because of the coffeepot, but I had seen it there when I visited her, too. I have the Rockwell sketch in my house as a prized possession. It is a wonderful likeness of a good friend drawn by another good friend.

Norman Rockwell is probably the best-known artist and illustrator in America. When a Rockwell cover appeared on the *Saturday Evening Post*, the magazine ran extra copies and consistently sold out. He produced over three hundred covers for the *Post*, and the book, *Norman Rockwell Artist and Illustrator*, at sixty dollars sold well in countries all over the world.

Norman Rockwell's work now spans a period of over sixty-five years. He did not set out to see how much money he could make. He said, "My idea of heaven is to have four assignments without a deadline." A story in *Graphics Magazine* stated that Rockwell has made a greater contribution to modern art than any other painter in his time. It went on to say that some artists who paint realistically are accused of copying photography — but Norman Rockwell improves on photography. He is without peer in his ability to depict life accurately and amusingly. Norman Rockwell will be remembered because he painted people as he saw them, and his art will be a history of our times.

My favorite Norman Rockwell painting is only indirectly related to our business. It came about as a result of a catastrophe. On Friday, July 13, 1951, Kansas City was struck by the most destructive flood in its history. The Missouri River overflowed into the industrial district. Government engineers assured us that our warehouses in the bottoms, where the Missouri and Kansas rivers met, were in no danger. Nevertheless, our people scrambled to move everything from the first to the second and third floors. About an hour after the government report, we were given ten minutes to evacuate because the dikes had given way.

Six to eight feet of water poured through our warehouses, washing away around a half-million dollars' worth of paper stock and Christmas cards. By the time I got to the scene, our supplies were rolling down the river like confetti. The flood had covered the railroad tracks for miles along the western approach to the city as well as the stockyards. Trees, trucks, box cars, parts of buildings and even carcasses of animals were flowing through the first floors of our warehouses. The power of the

166

flood was such that a railroad car weighing 23,000 pounds with a 50,000-pound load was washed away.

Television and newspaper reports gave the impression that the flood had wracked the main business district. The mistake was natural because the lowland along the rivers, essentially made up of warehouses, had been the main business district when Kansas City was young, and it was still known as "the Central Industrial District." I called Carl Byoir, head of our public relations firm in New York, to ask if he could do anything about correcting the story. By that evening the media reports were explaining the difference.

Norman Rockwell called from Vermont to ask if there was anything he could do. I thanked him and said there really wasn't. After I thought it over, I hurriedly called him back and asked if he could come to Kansas City to do a painting that would somehow show the city rebuilding after the flood. He agreed.

Norman donned high boots and set out trudging through the debris. He did a number of remarkable sketches. Then he returned home to produce an oil painting, almost life size, of a man with his sleeves rolled up, holding blueprints and surveying the ravaged city. We prepared a large brochure with the painting and the story of how the city had survived. The picture became known as "The Kansas City Spirit," symbolizing the indomitable courage of men and women who put service above self. It is one of Norman's best paintings and is proudly displayed in our headquarters today.

For many years I dreamed of having Winston Churchill's paintings on our greeting cards. It was an unlikely possibility. Churchill had given a few paintings to close friends but had only allowed one to be sold — at an auction to benefit the Young Women's Christian Association. But I decided we should at least give it a try.

Early in 1950 we sent an agent to London to see Churchill's solicitor, Anthony F. Moir. They discussed the proposal for about an hour, and Moir was frankly skeptical but agreed to call Churchill. He told him that an American company wished to publish his paintings on greeting cards. Churchill asked, "What company?" When he was told Hallmark, he replied, "That's a good firm. Make a deal with them." He hung up without giving any details on how he wanted it handled. After

167

(Overleaf) *Kansas City's Central Industrial District as it appeared during the height of the 1951 flood.*

J.C. Hall and Hallmark employees surveying flood damage to Hallmark warehouse facilities

Norman Rockwell called Joyce Hall to ask if there was anything he could do to help. Hall suggested he might come to Kansas City to do a painting depicting rebuilding. The result, "The Kansas City Spirit," is at right.

further discussion with our agent, Moir decided he would have to call Churchill again. This time Churchill said testily, "I told you to make a deal with them." And he hung up again.

The proposal we submitted was accepted immediately, and a contract was drawn for reproduction rights in this country to nine Churchill paintings. Shortly after, I received the following cable: "I am delighted at the opportunity of having my paintings exhibited through the medium of Christmas cards — Winston Churchill." We sent Elwood Whitney, the senior art director and vice president of our advertising agency, Foote, Cone & Belding, to England to select eighteen paintings — from which we would use nine. Instead, we asked to use twelve and were given permission.

The Association of Art Museum Directors was meeting in Kansas City when the paintings arrived. I called Laurence Sickman, assistant director of the Nelson Gallery, to offer our help in entertaining them. We had shown Churchill's paintings to Sickman, and he felt his guests would greatly enjoy seeing them as well. I invited them to a Sunday brunch. The paintings were not signed, and we thought it would be interesting to show them without immediately revealing the artist's name.

We simply told the curators that we were thinking of using the paintings on greeting cards and wanted their opinions. Among the group was the man who directed one of the largest museums in the country. After carefully examining each painting, he was the first to speak up: "Well, one thing is certain. Whoever the artist is, he's more than a Sunday painter." The others reflected his judgment, and some went considerably beyond that in their praise.

It was with some pleasure that we announced the artist was Winston Churchill. They were greatly surprised and agreed that it had been important to see the paintings without prejudice. Some had seen a few Churchill paintings reproduced in magazines, which had not done them justice. Now confronted with the actual work, they were amazed by his ability.

Soon after Donald graduated from college in 1950, he joined Elizabeth and me on a trip to Europe — and especially to England, where we had been invited to visit Winston Churchill at Chartwell, his country home.

We had corresponded but I had not met the man and was apprehensive about walking into his presence.

Our appointment was for lunch at one o'clock, and Anthony Moir made it clear that Churchill expected people to be on time. As we approached Chartwell, Churchill's car was just ahead of ours. We slowed down, waiting for him to enter the house.

We were shown to a large living room that had once been his studio. In less than ten minutes, Churchill had changed from a business suit to one of his familiar wartime "siren suits." He greeted us rather brusquely. I thought immediately that he *did* have the face of a baby and the jaw of a bulldog. It also struck me that he had very small hands.

He was clearly more solicitous of Elizabeth than the rest of us. He asked me, "Do you want Scotch or tomato juice?" I said tomato juice, and he poured a large glass. As I was about to reach for it, he drank it himself. I poured my own. He escorted Elizabeth to the dining room as we tagged along. I wondered if he was going to have anything to say to us.

Anthony had warned us he might be a bit abrupt at the beginning. Apparently this was when he sized people up. By the time the first course was underway, Churchill was becoming quite friendly. He turned to Elizabeth and said, "I've found that the best way to get my energy is in whiskey." Then he looked at Donald, who was only twenty-two, and added, "That is in the case of older men. It doesn't apply to young people who are getting regular exercise and have good appetites."

He asked me if we were disappointed in his paintings on our cards. I said we were delighted and sales had exceeded our highest forecast. In fact, we had already sold four and one-half million cards to our dealers in advance of the Christmas season, and they would be buying many more. "How many?" He wanted me to repeat the figure. He looked at me sharply, presumably to decide if I had exaggerated. "If you'd like to see them," I said, "I have samples of the cards with me." He immediately asked the butler to bring in my briefcase. He looked over the cards, and I could see he was pleased. His only criticism was that they flattered his paintings.

He proceeded to ask a number of questions, and I was amazed by his knowledge and curiosity. He wanted to know about the processes used in reproduction, how we distributed cards, when we shipped them, how many salesmen we had and how they operated. He asked how many cards would be sold by December 1, and what happens if they don't sell well? It was not difficult to understand how he arrived at decisions with his intense questioning about anything that interested him — and it seemed almost everything did.

The main course was chicken, and he grumbled about that. "I had enough chicken during the war to last me forever," he said. "And I'm still getting a lot more of it." He shouted for the butler, then asked him angrily why he hadn't filled the wine glasses. But he was pleased with the dessert, a thin raspberry custard served in a stemmed glass. He smiled and said something about "raspberry goop." As we reached for our spoons, he said, "I like goop" — and thereupon picked up his glass and drank it down.

I told him how the museum curators had reacted to his "anony-mous" work, and he became quite emotional. Sometime later, his daughter Sarah told me that a compliment about his painting pleased him more than anything said about his writing or even his statesmanship.

Our editorial and art departments had made an album dedicated to Winston Churchill, showing his twelve paintings along with a sixteen-line poem welcoming him to the Hallmark gallery of artists. As he read the poem, following along with his finger, he asked, "Who wrote this?" I said a young woman on our staff. He looked over the pages where our people had signed their names and said, "You have quite an organiza-tion." His voice cracked and tears came to his eyes. I think he hoped we hadn't noticed them. We were surprised and touched. Then the tears disappeared, and he slammed the album shut. His moods changed abruptly, but it was easy to see he was a deeply sentimental man.

He asked Elizabeth if she would like to tour the house and grounds. We just assumed the invitation included the rest of us and followed along. In almost every room there was one of his better paintings — only then would he turn to me to give a brief explanation of what he had tried to do, always pointing out the weakest element of the painting. He was giving me more credit as an art expert than I deserved. And it became clear how pleased he was to have his paintings reproduced for a vast American audience. He was also complimentary of the United States and Americans in general. I said that since I had just been to the continent, I wished more Europeans felt that way. With some surprise,

174

he replied, "Don't forget — I'm half American."

In his bedroom, he demonstrated a shelf that folded down from the wall over his bed, where he did much of his writing. He took special pleasure in showing us how his elaborate dictating apparatus operated when he was propped up in bed. I said that it must be a great convenience. He shrugged his shoulders and replied, "I don't even use the damn thing."

It was also in this room that he picked up an inscribed photograph of President Truman and asked if his home town of Independence was part of Kansas City. I explained that it was in the same county. Did I know the president? I told him I did. He must have sensed a lack of enthusiasm on my part, because he looked at me sharply and said, "When the history of our time is finally written, Harry Truman will go down as one of your greatest presidents." I later realized how right he was.

After completing the tour of the house, he took Elizabeth by the arm to go out to see the grounds. Chartwell is on 350 acres of beautiful, rolling English countryside. Churchill asked Elizabeth, "Would you like to see my brick wall?" He had actually built it himself and had even joined the bricklayer's union. He was even more proud of the rose garden bordering it, which I suspect he planned. On the Churchills' fiftieth wedding anniversary, their children had watercolor artists paint each variety of rose in the garden.

He marched us over to a fish pond he had also built to see his Golden Orfe. They're beautiful fish, much larger than goldfish — some more than a foot long. We were surprised to hear him call them "darlings," and they came to him immediately. He let out a bellow for "Thompson!" Walter Thompson, his valet, was always close at hand. He had also been Churchill's bodyguard during the war. He showed up with a can full of live maggots. Churchill pulled out a handful and threw them into the pond. The fish made away with them instantly. With the mischievous grin of a small boy, he asked Elizabeth if she would like to feed the fish. Much to his surprise, she held out her hand, and he plopped about a dozen maggots in it. He had obviously expected her to draw back, but Elizabeth was never squeamish about much of anything.

From the fish pond, Churchill led us to a small lake to see his black swans. He had been sent a pair from a friend in Australia, and a flock had developed since. Thompson was on the job with a loaf of bread. Churchill broke up pieces, and the swans were quick to come. He called them "darlings," too, and talked to them as if they would answer.

Down a hill from the lake we arrived at a small paddock to visit his favorite yearling. If any of his pets had names, we would never know it. The yearling was "darling" as well. He hugged the horse and patted him lovingly. Then he fed him bread while giving a pep talk about what he was expecting of him in a year or two — as a race horse. I learned later that his expectations were fully realized.

Churchill's affection for his "darlings" touched all of us. Sometime after our visit, a friend of his told me that one day Churchill was painting at Chartwell when he spotted a little robin. He intrigued the bird by making funny noises. Then he began feeding the robin daily until it would eat right out of his hand. As I listened to this story, I couldn't help but think that this was the man who had dared Hitler to cross the Channel when England had little left to fight with but courage, which he, more than anyone else, inspired — and this was the same man who could be so gentle with a little wild bird.

We climbed to a terrace and sat on a bench in the shade of a lovely old tree. I thought how grateful we would be to have a picture taken. I had a small camera with me — but enough sense to realize it was not my place to start taking snapshots. After resting a few minutes, Churchill said, "Where is that photographer?" By now we realized that someone always showed up when called. Sure enough, a photographer was on the spot. He took several pictures — and before we left London, there were photographs at our hotel signed by Churchill for each of us.

Churchill offered the men cigars, which we all promptly lit. We had been forewarned that he liked to see people smoke the cigars he gave out rather than put them away for souvenirs. The cigar was a man-sized Havana, and I found it a challenge to smoke much of it. But I was surprised to see Donald smoking like a veteran. I didn't even know he knew how.

Churchill asked if we would like to see his studio. It was a large room with all four walls covered with paintings. There must have been two or three hundred pictures. The lighting through gable windows was excellent. We examined the paintings for some time when Churchill opened a door to another room. There was a wooden rack about twenty feet long with two piles of unframed canvases stacked on it. There were still more canvases on a large table, some of them sticking together. I shuddered to think of them being allowed to deteriorate. I thought how much it would mean to me to own even the worst of the lot, but I had been told Churchill would part with a painting about as readily as he would with a child.

The afternoon was wearing on, and I had the feeling that Churchill was tiring. A jeep arrived, and he invited Elizabeth to ride back to the house with him. The rest of us walked. We had been over most of his estate, and Churchill had gone up and down the steep slopes with great energy. He was amazingly vigorous for a man of his age, then seventy-five. Less than a year later, he became prime minister of Great Britain once again.

By the time we had tea it was close to five. I had asked before how we would know when to leave and was told, "Don't worry — you'll know." When we finished tea, Churchill jumped up and said it was time for the nap his doctor prescribed every afternoon. He thanked us for publishing his paintings and asked us to sign his guest book. Then he bade us a warm goodbye and invited us to visit him again. I left with mixed feelings — being thrilled to have met Winston Churchill and let down to think that I probably would never see him again. I never dreamed there would be many more meetings over the next fifteen years.

It was entirely coincidental that I met Sarah Churchill shortly after receiving a cable from her father. It had been sent to me at the Beverly Hills Hotel in California when I was on a business trip concerning our radio program. The Beverly Hills Hotel is one of the finest I know and has a pleasant intimacy about it. After a couple of days, I always got to know the maids, the elevator operators and the bellmen.

When the maid entered our room one evening, she said that Sarah Churchill was also a guest at the hotel. She added that her suite was just down the hall from ours. It struck me as unusual for the maid to tell us this. But she said, "I just thought you might be interested." Then I picked up a folder that had Churchill's cable in it and started to hand it to her. She said, "Oh, I already read that."

A day or so later, the phone rang, and a man introduced himself as Anthony Beauchamp. The name didn't register, but fortunately he

Joyce, Elizabeth and Donald Hall with Sir Winston Churchill during their visit to Chartwell in 1950

(Facing page) *Joyce Hall with Sir Winston Churchill during Chartwell visit*

Letter to Hall from Sir Winston agreeing to a traveling exhibit of Churchill's paintings

NIGHTSBRIDGE 7972.

28, HYDE PARK GATE,
LONDON. S.W.7.

24 June, 1957.

My dear Mr Hall,

It was most agreeable to see you and Mrs. Hall again, and I enjoyed our conversation.

Following our meeting before your departure on June 20, I have decided that I should like to adopt your proposal. I should therefore be happy to make thirty of my pictures available to be shown at the different museums in America as you propose. I have written to the President accordingly in answer to his letter which you brought.

Perhaps you would let me know the name of a representative over here with whom I can get in touch when the pictures are chosen so that arrangements for their shipping and insurance can be made?

2.

Finally, please accept my warmest thanks for your thought in sending me the film of THE LARK. I look forward very much to seeing it at Chartwell.

Yours very sincerely,

Winston S. Churchill

Mr. Joyce Hall.

explained that he was Sarah Churchill's husband. I asked him how he knew I was in the hotel, and he said the maid had told him. She was a very busy lady.

That afternoon Elizabeth and I met with Sarah and her husband before she had to leave for a theater where she was playing the lead in *The Philadelphia Story*. She was pleased and surprised that her father had consented to using his paintings on greeting cards. The next evening we went to see the play as Sarah's guests and realized what a fine actress she was.

Less than a year later, after an extensive study, Fax Cone, the head of the advertising agency bearing his name, recommended that we do a weekly television show moderated by Sarah Churchill. It was widely assumed that this came about because we published her father's paintings, which was not the case at all. Sarah Churchill was an established actress in her own right, and she was also an intelligent and engaging personality. She had the advantage, too, of knowing countless people in all walks of life.

The show was called "Hallmark Presents Sarah Churchill," and her first guest was Eleanor Roosevelt. They had been good friends for years. When Mrs. Roosevelt entered the studio, she charmed everyone with her warmth and thoughtfulness. And of course, Mrs. Roosevelt was an old hand at this sort of show, but it was Sarah's first interview program — and she was extremely nervous. Mrs. Roosevelt recognized this immediately. She sat down with Sarah and put her arm around her. Sarah was in tears. Mrs. Roosevelt talked to her quietly for about ten minutes, telling her, "It's going to be all right, my dear. Don't worry. Just talk about things we know. You'll be fine." And Sarah was. In fact, she handled the interview like a veteran. We continued the show to the end of 1951, then started a program called "Hallmark Television Playhouse" with Sarah as the hostess. After only three weeks, we changed the name to "Hallmark Hall of Fame" — and some people think we changed television as well.

Elizabeth and I became very fond of Sarah. She was a sweet, friendly girl, and she was as devoted to her father as he was to her. In a wonderful little book she wrote, *A Thread in the Tapestry*, she expressed that relationship movingly. Sarah visited us frequently, and I especially remember one summer when she spent a week at our place in Grand Lake, Colorado. Elizabeth and I were concerned about how she'd take it since this would be much hardier living than Sarah was used to in England or the Riviera.

We met her at the airport in Denver and proceeded to the lake. There was no road to our house, so we had to go by boat. As we were crossing, a friend who had just won a sailing regatta approached us in his sailboat. We introduced Sarah to him and his family, and he invited her to sail to our home.

Sarah was delighted, even though she was wearing a heavy suit. She needed no help getting into the sailboat, which settled into a fairly still breeze. But within minutes an extremely rough mountain squall came up and caught the mainsail, flipping the boat over and dumping its passengers into the ice cold water. We came as close as we could to everyone while still avoiding the sails and riggings. Sarah had the longest distance to swim to our boat. She made it with ease, even with one of the youngest children under her arm. I was aware of Sarah's Churchillian temper and expected almost anything — but she climbed aboard, shivering and laughing. She thought it was a great initiation to her stay at Grand Lake.

Indirectly, Sarah Churchill was responsible for a gift that I value as much as anything I've ever received — an original painting by Sir Winston Churchill. Shortly after Sarah was at Grand Lake, she was having dinner with her father, then the prime minister. He commented that he had always wanted to do something special for me.

Sarah knew how much I cherished the thought of having one of her father's paintings — and she also knew that I would never consider asking for one or even asking to buy one. But Sarah approached her father with the subject — and he exploded in fine Churchillian style. Nothing more was said until after dinner.

Churchill called Sarah over to show her a painting he did of a beach scene on the island of Jamaica. He told her that if he was going to give me a painting it had to be one of his best. The next morning he had it packed for Sarah to take with her to the United States. It hangs over the fireplace in my office, and it means more to me than I can say. As far as anyone knows, it is the only Churchill painting that was done on this side of the ocean.

The Art of Sentiment

There have been many outstanding artists and writers associated with Hallmark over the years. However, this was not always the case. When we first started publishing greeting cards, we had only one artist on our staff who did all the designing. By 1925 we required the talents of a dozen artists, and today we employ more than three hundred artists with widely varying skills. In addition there are about half again as many working in specialized graphic techniques, such as lettering and retouching.

For many years, we had a small group of German artists, and we began to realize how important it was to have the influence of artists from other countries. This was particularly true of Japanese artists — not only for the delicate style of their work, but for their proficiency in certain techniques, such as water color. After World War II we brought in artists from Japan, England, Italy and Sweden. Over the years our staff has been a miniature United Nations of artists, representing some thirteen different nationalities.

This complex division of the company operates with amazing harmony, especially since 1939 when Jeannette Lee joined our organization as assistant to the design director after graduating cum laude from the University of Kansas City. A few years later she took full charge of the department. Today Jeannette is the corporate vice president, Corporate Design, as well as a member of the board of directors.

It is not easy to supervise the work of hundreds of creative people, producing thousands of new designs every year. By far the greatest volume of work is done in our own studios. But we don't hesitate to go outside for artwork that will add interest and quality to our cards.

Given our continued success with Walt Disney's characters, we also began using other comic strip figures — Blondie and Dagwood, Popeye, Dennis the Menace. And more recently, we introduced Charles Schulz's "Peanuts" gang to greeting cards and other products. Certainly Schulz is the cartoon champion of all time — and for greeting cards, too. He is a magician with a pencil. The simplicity of his drawings and the

182

unaffected frankness depicting everyday life give his characters an appeal the public never tires of.

In 1962 we received a letter from an unknown artist in Amarillo, Texas — Betsey Clark. She sent samples of her work, as thousands of others do, but not one in a thousand clicks. Betsey's characters are tender, little ragamuffin children and animals, which we call "Charmers." While a number of our people thought they were *too cute,* Jeannette Lee championed Betsey Clark's work and the public agreed enthusiastically.

Betsey's creations were introduced as a special promotion. In our terms, a "promotion" does not simply mean publicizing a product. It is a special theme for a group of cards that is featured separately from our regular lines.

Our first real promotion was in 1948 when we produced a set of sixteen "Storybook Dolls." They were designed by Vivian Trillow Smith, a wonderful artist on our staff. The dolls were cut out of cardboard and folded to stand up, with real feathers on their hats. They were all popular, but Cinderella was the favorite. The next year we added eight "Dolls of the Nations," such as Maria from Mexico, Katrinka of Holland and Ann of England. When Metro-Goldwyn-Mayer produced a new version of *Little Women,* they asked us to use the four leading characters for storybook dolls as they were played on the screen by June Allyson, Elizabeth Taylor, Margaret O'Brien and Janet Leigh.

For many years I approved every item that went into production at Hallmark, and I was particularly concerned about promotions. Frequently people would present an idea to me saying, "Here's something different." Then I'd tell them the story of a salesman who tried to sell me a gadget for our retail store that automatically knocked on the window to attract customers. It was "different", too. But I could also put a billy goat in the window and attract attention. It'd be different — and worse. Eventually our people got the idea that in developing new items they had to be different — and better.

In 1948 we started a line of Christmas cards under the imprint of Hallmark Gallery Artists. We brought to the public the work of Leonardo da Vinci, Michelangelo, Raphael, Rembrandt, Botticelli, Renoir, El Greco, Monet, Gauguin, Cezanne and Van Gogh. So, through

Early Hall Brothers' art staff

Jeannette Lee with artist in 1947

One of Hallmark's artists at work

In 1947, this "Okay Committee" reviewed each item produced by the company

Jeannette Lee reviewing artwork for greeting cards with J.C. Hall

PEANUTS
by SCHULZ

Charles M. Schulz'
Peanuts characters have appeared
on Hallmark products
for several years

PEANUTS Characters:
© 1950, 1958, 1965, 1966
United Feature Syndicate, Inc.

SCHULZ

BETSEY CLARK

Betsey Clark, the creator of a popular series of characters introduced in 1962

the "unsophisticated art" of greeting cards, the world's great masters were shown to millions of people who might otherwise not have been exposed to them.

Many fine artists who might seem unlikely for greeting cards have been published by us — Pablo Picasso, Andrew Wyeth, Georgia O'Keefe and Salvador Dali. Dali's painting, "The Last Supper," was especially memorable. On one occasion, I asked him to do a Santa Claus for us — and it was superb. But one element made it unusable for a greeting card — Dali had one of his melting watches hanging out of a drawer in Santa's stomach. Still it was a valuable painting.

Albert Skira's fine art books were probably the most comprehensive line with the most faithful reproductions of the works of the Old Masters and Impressionists. We used them on cards for a number of years. Skira also published a book for Hallmark, *The Spirit of the Letter in Painting*, which we supplied to libraries around the country and distributed in our best retail outlets.

In the 1930s we started using the art prints of Vivian Mansell of London. Mansell would come to the United States each year to show us his new work. During the war, he ran the blockade and made the long, difficult trip even though he was in his eighties. On his last trip it took him over three months to get back to London. I remember him fondly. One evening at the height of the war we were having dinner at the Muehlebach Hotel in Kansas City. Wine was scarce, and he asked if we could possibly get a bottle of Italian wine. I said, "Knowing your feelings about Mussolini, I didn't think you'd drink Italian wine." He smiled and said, "Well, I find it very effective to get a bottle of Chianti and drink to Mussolini's complete confusion."

Huldah, the artist whose work was similar to the French impressionists, began painting for us in 1950. Before meeting her, I expected to see a little French girl with large round eyes resembling some of her paintings. Instead, she was tall and statuesque, and when I said, "You're not French at all, are you?" she replied, "I certainly am not. I come from seven generations of Texans. In fact, my grandmother's uncle was Sam Houston." Startled, I replied quickly, "So was mine!" My grandmother's uncle was indeed Sam Houston. Her first reaction clearly was that I was making fun of her, but I convinced her I was serious.

For many years Saul Steinberg's sketches as well as his more traditional work have appeared on our cards. Most people think of him strictly as a cartoonist of social commentary because of his remarkable drawings in the *New Yorker*, but I have found that he is a serious artist of great stature.

We were determined to develop a program that would give greater exposure of fine art to the public. We sought the advice of our advertising agency, Foote, Cone and Belding. Fairfax Cone, the president, and Elwood Whitney felt we should attract artists and museums around the world. We wanted to build a mass audience for fine painting — and also provide more work for artists. A painting can make just as important a contribution to everyday living as a book, play or movie — provided enough people see it.

We announced Hallmark's International Art Awards Competition in 1948 and had almost ten thousand entries. The winning paintings were shown to record crowds in Paris — then were exhibited at the Wildenstein Galleries in New York. It was the largest collection of contemporary paintings ever presented at a single exhibition. For two years the exhibit toured major art museums around the country.

The first competition was for French and American artists, and we had a surprising number of entries from the great names in both countries. This was especially gratifying since Picasso had denounced the competition as anti-communist and had encouraged French artists not to participate. Ironically, a midwestern congressman denounced it as communist-inspired.

Fax Cone had told me a number of times that I should get acquainted with Henry Dreyfuss, the great industrial designer. Fax said, "He's the only man I know who is a professional shopper like you." In other words, Dreyfuss shopped for ideas, not purchases. I invited Dreyfuss to spend a day with us in Kansas City. After looking over our operation and meeting our crew of artists, he didn't see how he could be of much service. However, in getting to know him, I was convinced he could make a great contribution by bringing new ideas to us and improving old ones.

Henry was on our consulting staff from the early 1960s until his untimely death in 1972. He had the most creative mind I've ever known. It ran as smoothly and effectively as a Rolls Royce engine. His personality was equal to his ability. He was wonderful to be with — in spite of the fact that he left you mentally, though pleasantly, exhausted. He contributed taste, beauty and quality to all our endeavors.

Photography came into its own in the competition to produce fine greeting cards. We began developing a staff of outstanding photographers and using the work of many free-lancers as well. As far back as the 1930s we gave a promising young Kansas City photographer his first assignment. We sent him to New England to shoot winter scenes of old country churches. He produced a remarkable set of pictures. Later he became one of *Life* magazine's most famous war photographers. And he has done several brilliant books — among them, *Picasso's Picasso*, *The Kremlin* and *War Without Heros*. His name, of course, is David Douglas Duncan.

While we certainly give a lot of attention to the graphics and design of our cards, we are just as concerned about the message — or, as we say, the sentiment. A well-known axiom around Hallmark is that a card is picked up by a customer for what it looks like but is purchased for what it says — which determines whether it serves its purpose or not.

Writing sentiments is a highly specialized skill. The general opinion is that it's easy. Writers in other fields especially assume that greeting card sentiments can be dashed off in the shower. We receive as many as 2,500 free-lance submissions a month and publish less than one percent of them.

What a sentiment says is extremely important, but even more important is how it's said. With few exceptions, sentiments should not be long and should be understood immediately. People who have the ability to say what they feel simply and in a pleasing way are the best greeting card writers.

Often people say they do not want sentimental cards. But our experience is that they will choose the sentimental card when it's properly done. Greeting cards are sent to special people in their lives, for whom they have strong feelings — parents and relatives, sweethearts and friends. These intense relationships require sentimental language.

A good sentiment writer must be able to put himself in the position of both sender and recipient. In judging cards we often ask "What is its sendability?" The best-written sentiment and the handsomest design are meaningless if they don't fit a sending situation. Since there are millions of senders and receivers, we have to determine the most effective combinations of sentiments and designs. All of our

190

cards are compared on a sales basis in thousands of stores and run through our computers. One of our greatest assets is our file of tested and proven sentiments.

Over many years of experience, we have found that the vast majority of greeting card buyers prefer verse to prose. One reason may be tradition. The first published sentiments were in verse, which became so well established that a greeting card did not seem to be a greeting unless it rhymed. Probably another reason is that verse is more difficult to write and adds value to the greeting. Also, verse is recognized as romantic language — and more appropriate to occasions for sending cards. People can express emotions in verse that might seem embarrassing in prose.

We publish prose, of course, in our humorous contemporary line, many sympathy cards, Christmas greetings and cards for men. We've also introduced more prose in cards directed to young adults, illustrated with soft-focus, romantic photography.

People ask me who writes our sentiments. In fact, over the years, I've often been asked if I was a writer or an artist. People assume I must be one or the other — but I am neither. I have never drawn much more than a straight line, and I've never even tried to write a sentiment. The overwhelming majority of our sentiments are written by members of our staff. They are a talented and prolific group. It is tough work, but it's very rewarding. Our writers see their work published on millions of greeting cards that reach many more millions of people since each card is shared by at least two individuals — and usually more.

We also use quotations and poetry from a varied group of outside sources, such as Archibald MacLeish, Boris Pasternak, Phyllis McGinley, Ogden Nash, Norman Vincent Peale and Fulton J. Sheen. And we use selective writings from many great literary figures — William Shakespeare, Elizabeth Barrett Browning, Charles Dickens, Walt Whitman, John Keats, Emily Dickinson, Mark Twain and Ralph Waldo Emerson.

One of the most demanding tasks in publishing greeting cards is not only writing them but proofreading. Can you imagine a spelling error in a greeting card? A newspaper, magazine or even a book can have misspellings and still sell — but not a greeting card. Hallmark cards go through at least ten proofreadings. If one letter is wrong, the entire run is thrown out at a cost of thousands of dollars. But seldom does the

44th Parallel, Andrew Wyeth

Nun, Robert Vickrey

Veronica, Elaine de Kooning

Two Against the White, Charles Shuler

STEINBERG

The work of Saul Steinberg appeared
on Hallmark products for many years

STEINBERG

MADONNA AND CHILD   LEONARDO DA VINCI

1.

2

4.

Albert Skira's fine art reproductions were used on cards for a number of years

1. Leonardo da Vinci
2. Sandro Botticelli
3. Pieter Brueghel, the Elder
4. Detail, The Coronation of the Virgin, Louvre, Paris
5. Paul Klee
6. Bernard Buffet

THE CANAL SAINT - MARTIN, PARIS   BERNARD BUFFET

197

Edgar Guest, author of the poem that became one of the favorite sentiments on Hallmark cards for over fifty years

For My Friend

Merry Christmas

My Friend

I'd like to be the sort of friend that you have been to me
I'd like to be the help that you've been always glad to be
I'd like to mean as much to you each minute of the day
As you have meant old friend of mine to me along the way

I'm wishing at this Christmas time that I could but repay
A portion of the gladness that you've strewn along my way
And could I have one wish this year this only would it be
I'd like to be the sort of friend that you have been to me

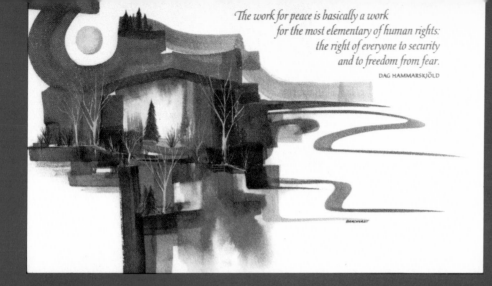

The work for peace is basically a work
for the most elementary of human rights:
the right of everyone to security
and to freedom from fear.

DAG HAMMARSKJÖLD

At left, a timeless poem, "A Friend's Greeting" by Edgar Guest, has been used on our cards (bottom, the first usage and top right, in 1978) for more than fifty years. Many years of experience has proven that card buyers prefer verse to prose. Many people find it easier to use cards than to write something themselves, and they can express strong feelings in verse that might seem inappropriate in prose.

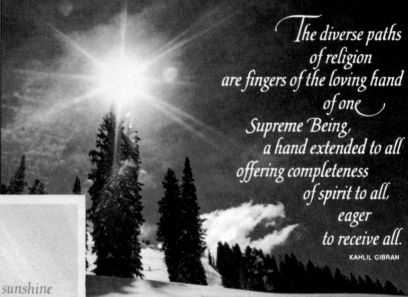

The diverse paths
of religion
are fingers of the loving hand
of one
Supreme Being,
a hand extended to all
offering completeness
of spirit to all,
eager
to receive all.

KAHLIL GIBRAN

While You're Ill...

Keep your face to the sunshine
and you cannot see the shadow.

Helen Keller

The overwhelming majority of sentiments are written by Hallmark staff members, however quotations from a varied group of authors, past and present, are used to fill public demand and interest in fine poetry.

199

Alexander Girard, designer

Girard with J.C. Hall

*In 1962, the William Rockhill Nelson
Gallery of Art exhibited the Girard folk
art collection. "The Nativity"
exhibition was sponsored by Hallmark
Cards, Inc., for the benefit of
People to People.*

company have more than six or seven typographical errors a year out of many millions of cards issued each day.

There have been a few classics. Not long ago, the title of a card read: "Congratulations on Your New Venture." As it went into printing, it read: "Congratulations on Your New Denture." Another card carried the title message: "Married all these years and what have you got to show for it?" The inside page was to read, "Me! Happy Anniversary, Mom and Dad." Instead, the page was totally blank, implying of course that they had nothing to show for it. Ironically, it sold so well that after correcting it, we reverted back to the blank card.

The process of producing a single greeting card, however, is not merely the successful collaboration of an artist and a writer. Thousands of people may be involved in hundreds of separate processes that contribute to the conception and publication of one card. Our cards may be flocked, flittered, coated, dyed, glued, laminated, embossed, die cut, engraved and glossed. They may be treated to look like leather, suede, wood, satin, cloth or metal. They may be permeated with oil, wood grain, cellulose fibers, colored threads or diamond-dust sequins. And if we can't find the right paper, our technicians create it; if we can't find the right ink, we make it ourselves.

The war years brought many changes in our business. And, surprisingly, it was the war in Europe that lead to a great advance in the quality of our printing. It had become apparent that the process that would be the backbone of our line was offset lithography.

Early in 1940 the receptionist called to say there was a man who wanted to see me to discuss lithography. The gentleman had an extraordinary tale. He said he was a German Jew from Munich named Hans Archenhold. He was the son-in-law of the principal owner of the biggest and best greeting card plant in Europe. Hitler had sent him and members of his family to a concentration camp, Dachau, and the Nazis had taken over the plant to build Messerschmidt fighter planes. Colonel Josiah Wedgewood of the famous Wedgewood china family had helped Archenhold escape from Germany. Hans was in London where he saw the Hallmark display at Selfridge's, the department store. Then and there he decided he wanted to work for us and came directly to Kansas City from London.

Archenhold had photographs of the plant in Munich, and he said he was known by the president of one of our large suppliers. His story proved to be accurate in every detail. He was recognized in the lithographic industry as one of the top men in Germany, a country famous for fine lithography. He had the highest standards of quality and had worked continuously to improve the lithographic process. I liked Hans and asked him to join our organization.

When this country got into the war, I called Hans and the heads of our production departments together. I warned them that the quality of goods being manufactured in the nation would be going down considerably, and unless we made a special effort, we would be affected as well. I challenged them to maintain and even improve our quality. With wartime restrictions this was like asking for a miracle. But the quality of our work actually did improve during this period.

We design and build some of our own color cameras, just as we do a great deal of the other equipment used in our plants. The cameras we use are not the kind you see around the necks of tourists. They range up to twenty feet long and take pictures forty-eight by forty-eight inches in size. These custom cameras have added to the continuing improvement of our art reproduction processes. Over the years we have introduced many other processes to our production program. Today I know of no quality graphic arts process that we do not have, some of which we developed ourselves and use exclusively.

A few years ago I was in Munich with Hans to attend a graphic arts fair. He took me to one of the largest graphic arts educational institutions in Germany. When we met the director, Hans said we had come to find out what was new in lithography. The director's reply was memorable — he said, "When we want to find out what is new in lithography, we contact Kansas City." That was the measure of the contribution Hans has made to our lithographic processes. Although Hans retired in July of 1970, he is a valued consultant and maintains close ties with our operation.

During World War II when there was a dire shortage of paper, the government dismissed the greeting card industry as non-essential in issuing priorities for paper. Edward L. Bernays, a legendary public relations executive, was engaged to develop a plan to inform the public and the government of the importance of greeting cards, especially during wartime. Before the study, Bernays himself regarded greeting cards as simply a novelty with no social significance. He learned some things we didn't know ourselves — or at least hadn't thought about.

He found that greeting cards were one of the most important means of personal communication. Over half of all personal correspondence was represented by greeting cards, and they had taken on even more meaning with so many people separated from their families. The survey showed that greeting cards were a much-needed way of expressing deeply felt sentiments during trying times. It is not easy for most people to write sentimental or sympathetic letters even under normal circumstances. Greeting cards were the natural substitute. Bernays concluded that greeting cards were a major "factor in building the morale of the people...I have no doubt about the useful purpose they serve in a society in which there are now millions less lonely because of them."

As a result, greeting cards were in much greater demand during the war than ever before. Women had always been natural users of cards — now men who had never sent them before turned to them in droves. The two great wars, which separated families around the globe, broadened the custom of sending greeting cards.

We realized many years ago that ours was a sensitive business. The shared sentiment a greeting card represents opens lines of communication that might otherwise be closed. A greeting card can create, enhance and often rebuild friendships and associations. Samuel Johnson once wrote: "A man, Sir, should keep his friendships in constant repair." This has become increasingly difficult in our complex and mobile society.

In the late 1930s I met a young university president who had worked his way through school in a bookstore where greeting cards were sold. He had watched countless people select cards. They would study the designs and read the sentiments with great care, then compare one card with another. He said he knew of no other product where there were as many items to select from. And unlike other products, few people can buy a card for someone else to send because it so strongly reflects the personality and taste of the sender.

Every day people by the millions gain the experience of making decisions about design, color and words — and, in that sense, they are making meaningful social and aesthetic statements, helping to set national standards of taste.

PART IV:
GOOD TASTE IS GOOD BUSINESS

A Winning Slogan

Hall Brothers had been the name of our company almost from its start in 1910. Somehow it had never been satisfactory to me. It sounded old fashioned.

One name had been on my mind since I first read about it in the early twenties in a story about the goldsmiths of fourteenth-century London. A mark had been adopted for each member of Goldsmiths Hall guaranteeing the purity of every gold and silver article made. It was called a "hall mark." The word fascinated me. It not only said quality in an authoritative way, but it also incorporated our family name.

It was difficult to sell the idea to most of the people in our organization. Understandably, they felt that a lot of work had gone into establishing a reputation for our product name. My feeling was that "hall mark" still identified our cards with Hall Brothers.

Finally, in 1928, we began using Hallmark on the back of every card. We got some complaints from our sales organization and a few dealers, but we received many more compliments. The public immediately began identifying our cards with the name. In 1949 we changed our symbol from a torch and shield to a five-point crown, and our advertising referred to Hallmark and the crown on the back of the cards.

I encountered resistance once again when I wanted to change our corporate name to Hallmark. Some of our people thought we'd actually lose our position in the industry. We didn't make that change until 1954, although our dealers and the public had long since referred to us as Hallmark Cards. Now it seems that our cards — and our company — have always been called Hallmark.

Advertising had always interested me. I pored over magazine ads when I was a boy working in my brothers' bookstore. And in the 1920s, when Americans started using greeting cards in greater numbers, I felt they should be told about the custom in some important way. We ran our first national ad, a full page I wrote myself, in the *Ladies' Home Journal* in 1928.

By the mid-thirties we started talking to advertising agencies about a program. None of them were enthusiastic, and a good many frankly said they were not even interested. The few willing to explore the idea said that our name and trademark would have to be on the front of the cards to make an advertising campaign pay off. This, of course, was unthinkable — people weren't buying advertisements, they were buying greeting cards. One agency head told me: "You'll never be able to advertise greeting cards if you expect people to turn them over and read the name." Another said: "Greeting cards can't be sold for a brand name like other products." And one man was more emphatic: "You can't afford to justify the expense of advertising." Our competitors felt the same way, as well as most of the people in our own organization.

After a discouraging time, I had lunch with the president of a small, progressive agency. He said that if our product and distribution were strong enough — compared to that of our competition — national advertising would be feasible. He believed that any product could be advertised successfully with this combination and the right agency. We experimented by advertising in one area, Chicago, where we had solid distribution.

The agency — Henri, Hurst and McDonald — recommended an established radio personality on WMAQ, Tony Wons, who chatted and read poems and quotations to his listeners. The format was a natural for greeting cards. In October, 1938, "Tony Wons' Radio Scrapbook" went on the air three times a week. Tony talked informally and read sentiments from Hallmark cards — and at the end he would add, "Look on the back for the identifying mark — a Hallmark card."

A few weeks before Christmas, Tony received a letter from an elderly woman, Mary McDonnell, in the Cook County Nursing Home. She wrote that his show was one of the few pleasures she had in life — she was alone in the world and hoped Tony would send her a Christmas card.

It was typical of Tony to go out of his way to visit her. On his next program he referred to her as "Grandma McDonnell" and read her letter. He said he was going to send her a Christmas card and suggested his listeners do the same. More than twenty thousand people responded — not only with cards, but gifts as well, addressed to "Grandma McDonnell." A special room had to be set aside in the home to accommodate everything.

The experience with this show convinced us to get into national advertising. The Tony Wons show went on network radio early in 1940. Rollie toured the country and reported back that "our radio program is the biggest thing that's ever happened in greeting cards."

Dealers began featuring Hallmark cards in their local advertising. Customers turned cards over, looking for the Hallmark emblem. Even cards displayed on cardboard mountings were pulled loose to check the back of them. There were a few complaints from dealers, especially those who didn't carry Hallmark cards and found their customers rejecting other brands. I even received homemade cards from children, who would fold a piece of paper, inscribe a message on the front and draw a Hallmark crown on the back. The entire industry benefited — the sale of greeting cards generally increased.

With the start of World War II, we began a network program called "Meet Your Navy," featuring the chorus of the Great Lakes Naval Training Center and a notable banjo player, Eddie Peabody. The show gained a wide audience and popularized the slogan "Keep 'em Happy With Mail."

By 1944 the attitude of advertising agencies toward Hallmark had changed considerably. Now we had the pick of any agency — but we didn't want the largest, we wanted the best. We boiled the choice down to three major ones. The first agency I called on was dominated by a single, sizeable account. It struck me that we could be little more than second fiddle there. The next agency had a great deal in its favor — an impressive record with many excellent accounts. However, I was to give them short shrift.

While I was talking with the president, a shoe shine boy put his head in the door. He noticed me and turned to leave. He had better manners than the executive, who looked down at his shoes and called the boy back. Without excusing himself, he swung around in his chair and proceeded to have his shoes shined with his back to me, while continuing to tell me why his agency should have the job. He didn't even have the courtesy to offer me a shine — and I needed one. I thought that a man that insensitive would not do a good job creating the right atmosphere for advertising Hallmark cards.

This was all for the best, because my third appointment was with Fairfax Cone of Foote, Cone & Belding. And I immediately liked Fax Cone. He said that he and his partners would like to visit Kansas City to see our operation. It occurred to me that if the top men of an organization wanted to make this kind of personal presentation, they must know a lot about advertising — and public relations.

About a week later Emerson Foote, Fairfax Cone and Donald Belding arrived in Kansas City. Before the day was over we knew this was the right agency. Fax Cone would handle our account personally — and I was convinced he could develop a quality program to sell a quality product.

After a few years I asked Fax to recommend a public relations agency. He didn't hesitate suggesting Carl Byoir & Associates. Carl Byoir's name rang a bell, though I couldn't remember why. When he came to see me, he immediately said, "Joyce, how good to meet you again." Years before, I had spent a weekend in Des Moines, Iowa, visiting a friend, Walter "Stub" Steward, a prominent lawyer who had been an all-American quarterback at the University of Iowa. Another guest was a friend of Stub's from college days — Carl Byoir. In fact, Stub had financed Carl's first year in school. By the second year, Byoir had started a clothes cleaning and pressing operation for students and was making more than enough money to pay Stub back and put himself through college.

Byoir was a fascinating man. He had been close to President Woodrow Wilson and had attended the Versailles peace conference at the President's request. After World War I, he was instrumental in promoting Czechoslovakia's model declaration of independence working with the great Czech patriot Tomas Masaryk. He got the cooperation of President Franklin D. Roosevelt in raising more than a million dollars in one night to fight infantile paralysis. And he had developed one of the largest public relations agencies in the world.

Now, in meeting him again in 1948, I said that I was looking for the kind of public relations man who had changed the image of Stephens College, a girls' school in Columbia, Missouri. I had been told that

210

Stephens was having trouble financially. They hired a public relations man who managed to get a story in the *Saturday Evening Post* showing that more Stephens girls got married within a year or two after college than girls from any other school in the country. This resulted in a great increase in enrollment. Carl Byoir just smiled, but his associate looked like the cat who'd swallowed the canary. He said, "Well, then, you might want to hire Carl, because he did that job."

Carl Byoir was the greatest public relations man I have ever known and a brilliant businessman. When he became ill and "retired" to Florida, he made another fortune in real estate. There simply wasn't anything he couldn't do.

For many years we tried to come up with a slogan that would do the best job advertising Hallmark cards. We started with "Hallmark Cards Say What You Want to Say, the Way You Want to Say It" — which was quite a mouthful. On the Tony Wons program, we used, "Look for the Hallmark and Crown on the Back of the Card." But these were entirely geared to promoting a brand name without emphasizing quality.

Ed Goodman, who was responsible for advertising and sales, put together a number of slogans that were more like a commercial than a single message. His original draft, on a three-by-five-inch card, appeared as follows:

> Three little words that mean so much — a Hallmark Card
> — They tell your friends you cared enough to send the very best
> — They best reflect your perfect taste...your thoughtfulness.
> So...Before you buy — Look on the back for those
>   three identifying words...A HALLMARK CARD

We began picking out bits and pieces. For several years we used "Hallmark Cards Best Reflect Your Perfect Taste, Your Thoughtfulness." Ed wanted to emphasize *caring* as the key to the slogan. And there it was — buried in the various phrases we had been using. In 1944 we adapted it to read: "When You Care Enough to Send the Very Best."

While we thought we had only established a good advertising slogan, we soon found out we had made a business commitment as well. The slogan constantly put pressure on us to make Hallmark cards "the very best." We have thrown away many millions of cards that did not justify that commitment. I somehow feel that without the slogan our products would not have been as good. And there is no question that the slogan had a favorable effect on the buying public.

In a survey made several years ago of twelve prominent advertising slogans, five out of six people were able to identify "When You Care Enough to Send the Very Best" with Hallmark products. It was second only in recognition to Coca Cola's "The Pause that Refreshes," which, to my astonishment, was eventually dropped. In 1977 our slogan rated first in a credibility survey conducted by the Bruskin people.

When the war was nearing an end, we began making plans with Foote, Cone & Belding for a new radio program. We engaged Charlotte Greenwood, a popular actress and comedienne famous for her long legs and high kicks. But she was the type of performer the public had to see as well as hear. We decided we needed a different format altogether. In 1946 we started "The Radio *Reader's Digest*," dramatizing stories from the magazine with the largest circulation in the world. But the identification with Hallmark got lost, and the *Reader's Digest* material, which had already been condensed, was difficult to adapt.

After a couple of years we asked the distinguished English novelist James Hilton, the author of *Lost Horizon* and *Goodbye, Mr. Chips*, to emcee a program featuring his and other stories. Fax Cone was so enthusiastic about the series that later he said of it, "Hallmark began to make history in broadcasting."

During Kansas City's centennial year in 1950, Hilton, along with Jane Wyman and Robert Young, came to the city to do a dramatization of its history. It was one of our best shows. Hilton fell in love with Kansas City. He said it was one of the most beautiful and historic cities in the country. He was so inspired that he planned to write a book about Kansas City, but his health did not hold up long enough for him to do it. James Hilton greatly influenced us in our goal to produce quality entertainment.

Lionel Barrymore took over as emcee, and a whole new adventure in broadcasting began that would eventually lead to television and "The Hallmark Hall of Fame." Barrymore was one of the most interesting and likeable men I have ever known. He was in a wheelchair, but he still drove his own car. He would wheel out to the car, put the chair in the trunk, then pull himself along the side of the car to the front seat.

When we hired him, he had not been doing much work because of his disability. I first met him at a dress rehearsal. He had been working all day and was taking a short break. I knew he had done some good etchings and thought we could use them on Christmas cards. I asked rather hesitantly, "Mr. Barrymore, would you consider letting us publish some of your etchings on greeting cards?" He slapped his hands on the arms of the wheelchair, looked up and said, "Hall, I'll do anything you want me to do." That was his way of saying thanks for giving him work when he needed it badly.

A few years later I got acquainted with the great character actor Edward Arnold. Long before he started acting, Arnold had been Lionel and John Barrymore's agent. I'll never forget how he characterized them. He said, "John was a gentleman roughneck, and Lionel was a roughneck gentleman."

Even after Lionel became very ill, he continued to emcee our show without a word of complaint. And he did as fine a job as anyone in good health. His agent told me that sixty days before the Christmas show — when he always read Charles Dickens's *Christmas Carol* — Lionel said, "I won't be able to do the show this year." He was asked why — and Lionel replied, "I won't be around." Shortly before Christmas, at the home where he spent his final days, he asked to be moved to a window where he could watch the sunset. He was taken back to bed, and he died.

With Lionel Barrymore's death, we left radio and began experimenting with television. The passing of the roughneck gentleman — one of the finest figures of the American theater and one of the greatest talents ever associated with Hallmark Cards — also marked the end of the time when people just heard about our products through advertising. Now America would see them, too.

"To Send the Very Best"

In the early 1920s, it was our family's custom to go for a ride on hot summer evenings. On one such occasion, we came upon a crowd listening to something very attentively — a radio. At that time, all I'd ever heard was a crystal set. I thought then, and I kept thinking through the years of radio and then television, that here was the opportunity for the whole world to learn. One man could reach millions. When television first appeared, I was convinced it was the greatest educational and entertainment medium the world had ever known. But as we know, that potential is still to be realized.

I didn't like what I heard on radio over the years, and I didn't like what I saw on television either. Fax Cone and I thought alike about the kind of shows we wanted to represent Hallmark Cards on the "Hall of Fame." We wanted shows that would not only be top entertainment but top quality as well. We wanted shows that would be appreciated by the entire family, and we wanted people to feel they had benefited from the time spent watching them.

We soon found out that knowing what you want on television is one thing and getting it is quite another. With the exception of Fax Cone, just about everybody had the same advice. We were cautioned against sponsoring shows that were "not in the popular vein," whatever that meant. But Fax and I were convinced that the American public was more interested in quality than some people in television realized. We were also convinced that the average American did not have the mind of a twelve-year-old, which many people in television seemed to feel. We didn't set out to get the largest audience on television — we wanted the best. We wanted *thinking* people to watch our shows — the people other people follow. And we wanted to reach the upper masses, not just the upper classes.

I've been quoted a number of times as saying I don't worry about ratings. That's not altogether true. I do worry about ratings, but I worry more about the show. I'd rather hold the attention of twenty-five million people than just "reach" fifty million. And I've never believed that people

214

who are watching your show are necessarily buying your products. The difference in our thinking is that we feel we need a combination of a good program, a good product *and* a good rating to get good results.

We also insisted that our advertising reflect our slogan. When you are selling what is basically a social custom, it must be on a high level. People want to reach up for a social custom, not down. Our policy for commercials was a simple one — they had to be just as tasteful as the show itself. From the beginning, this eliminated singing commercials and silly or slapstick ones that are all too common on television. We were also opposed to a "hard sell" because people watching our show were our guests. After all, it's not how loudly you shout your commercials, but how good your programs are — and, of course, the quality of your products.

It may be that if more of the early sponsors of quality television had held out a little longer, they might have been agreeably surprised. At times in the early days we, too, had our doubts, but striving for excellence always prevailed. If we had followed "expert" advice or had let ratings alone dictate our planning or had been panicked by adverse criticism, we would have deserved all the obscurity that by now probably would have been ours.

Through the years we established standards for our shows: They must have importance and lend balance and diversity to the entire season. Classic plays, original plays and long-run Broadway hits frequently appear on the "Hall of Fame" because they meet those standards. It took several years of experimenting to come up with a format for the "Hall of Fame" that satisfied us — and the public.

Early in December, 1951, Foote, Cone & Belding was contacted by NBC about finding a sponsor for an original opera written for television that the network had commissioned for Christmas. Our marketing people were right in feeling that it was too late to sponsor a program for our Christmas sales period. And it was argued that an opera was hardly the type of show to get much attention on television. Also, it was an hour long, making it expensive to sponsor. But I felt we could use the show to thank all the people who bought Hallmark cards. It was televised Christmas Eve.

The opera was Gian Carlo Menotti's *Amahl and the Night Visitors*

— and it was a beautiful show. We received thousands of letters, cards and telegrams thanking us for presenting it. The opera was beloved by adults and children alike and acclaimed by critics as a Christmas classic. *The New Yorker* called it "a lovely and wonderful thing to see and hear."

The moving story of the lame boy, Amahl, with Menotti's magnificent music, was so successful we repeated it by popular demand at Easter the next year in spite of its Christmas theme. Then we found ourselves showing it again at Christmas. In 1953 it became the first sponsored network show to appear in color. We presented *Amahl and the Night Visitors* seven times. And even then it was picked up by other sponsors and continues to be shown at Christmas.

Another milestone in the "Hall of Fame" was to come about under unusual circumstances. In 1953 I was at the Plaza Hotel in New York when Ed Cashman, a broadcasting executive at Foote, Cone & Belding, came to see me just as I was packing to catch the Twentieth Century Limited to Chicago. It was less than fifteen minutes before I had to leave.

Ed had an option from NBC to produce a special two-hour version of *Hamlet* based on Maurice Evans's famous *G.I. Hamlet*, which Evans had taken to military bases overseas. The option expired at midnight that night, so there was no chance to consult anyone. It seemed like a long shot. No one had presented a Shakespearean play on television before, no one had produced a show longer than an hour and no single sponsor had supported two hours of TV time on one show.

Ed continued to discuss the idea as I checked out of the hotel; then he followed me to a cab. I suggested he ride with me to the station. The train was right on time, and as I jumped aboard, I gave him the okay to go ahead with the show.

Hamlet made television history — directed by George Schaefer with a superb cast, including Maurice Evans, Sarah Churchill, Ruth Chatterton and Barry Jones. The production represented a number of "firsts" in television. The show established the concept of the TV special. It was also the first two-hour production and the first Shakespearean play to appear on television. But perhaps the most important first was that *Hamlet* was seen that April Sunday by more people than had seen it in the 350 years since it had been written.

The so-called TV "spectacular" had been born — that is a show of more than one hour that pre-empts a regularly scheduled program. It was ideal from our standpoint with our emphasis on seasonal selling. As a result, we decided we would buy television time only when we needed it most — just before our major selling seasons rather than an inflexible schedule of weekly time periods. And while one network accepted our experiment, we were told that the industry would never go for it on a permanent basis. I'm convinced that changing the standard practice of buying time on television had more to do with improving its quality than any other single factor. Perhaps the largest percentage of the best shows on television have been specials.

Our experience with *Amahl* and *Hamlet* also convinced us that we had found the ideal format to complement our products. We concluded that a longer-than-usual dramatic show produced with taste and quality dominates the evening on which it appears, increases viewer anticipation, is remembered longer and actually makes news. These shows also confirmed our feeling that the American public has high standards when it comes to identifying and appreciating quality.

A few of our dealers complained that the shows were too highbrow for selling greeting cards. One dealer wrote, "Shakespeare isn't helping bring customers into our stores." And the audiences were relatively small compared to those drawn by westerns and quiz shows.

But we were determined to stick with our programming concept. And it wasn't long before the "Hall of Fame" was winning larger audiences. By 1959 I was able to tell our dealers that an average of thirty-five million people were watching each show, advertised as "coming to you with the compliments of the fine stores where you buy Hallmark cards." And less than a year later, with the production of Shakespeare's *The Tempest*, the "Hall of Fame" became one of television's top ten shows with a total audience of over forty million.

Perhaps a sponsor should not have favorite shows and favorite performers, but should value his productions solely for their prestige — and the sale of his products. Well, I am a sponsor, but I am also as much a fan of the "Hall of Fame" as its most ardent follower. In fact, I have been a wide-eyed fan of the theater since I made my first trip to New York in 1910 — which was a trip to Broadway as much as to the big city. The advantage I have over other fans is that I can get in on the act, so to speak. While I was president of Hallmark, I read

Joyce C. Hall with Helen Hayes and Sarah Churchill

With Lynn Fontanne

Honoring George Schafer for his 50th Hallmark Hall of Fame production; Celeste Holm, right.

(Facing Page) First Emmy presented by National Academy of Television Arts and Sciences to a sponsor.

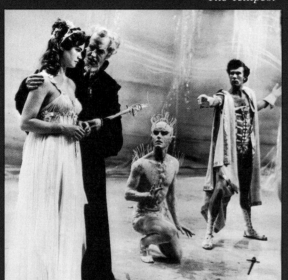

"The Tempest"

"Little Moon of Alban"

"Gideon"

"Amahl and the Night Visitors"

"The Magnificent Yankee"

"Teacher, Teacher"

"Victoria Regina"

"The Price"

221

every script and reserved the right of approval. Elizabeth read the scripts as well, always commenting on them constructively, and we never missed seeing a show, then discussing it in detail.

After *Hamlet*, Maurice Evans became something of a regular on the "Hall of Fame." He starred in five more Shakespearean productions: *Richard II, Macbeth, The Tempest, The Taming of the Shrew* and *Twelfth Night*. He also played leads in three of our George Bernard Shaw productions, *The Devil's Disciple, Man and Superman* and *Saint Joan*. Then in 1958 he brought his own Broadway success to the Hall of Fame, *Dial M for Murder*.

Among the first ladies of the "Hall of Fame," Julie Harris belongs in the forefront. In 1958 she had a great deal to do with making *Little Moon of Alban* a landmark production for us. In this original play for television, she gave such an extraordinary performance that there was little hope for any other actress to receive the Emmy award that year. She won, as did the play — for the best single dramatic program, best direction by George Schaefer, and best writing by James Costigan. The show also won four Sylvania Awards, the George Foster Peabody Award and the Christopher Award. Fax Cone said of the play, "In my opinion and the opinion of the television industry, *Little Moon of Alban* was the most original television program that has ever been aired."

Julie Harris had starred in two previous "Hall of Fame" shows — *The Good Fairy* in 1956, and in 1957 she repeated her Broadway triumph in *The Lark*. She continued to be our most honored actress in such shows as *Johnny Belinda, A Doll's House, Pygmalion, The Holy Terror, Anastasia* and the unforgettable *Victoria Regina*, which won three Emmys including best actress and "Program of the Year."

Helen Hayes became another favorite of ours. A sweet and totally unspoiled lady, she appeared in our productions of *Ah, Wilderness* by Eugene O'Neill, *The Cradle Song* and *Harvey*. In 1963, when Miss Hayes and Maurice Evans were touring with Shakespearean readings, they stayed with us in Kansas City and joined me in watching *Pygmalion* on the "Hall of Fame." We had recently done *Victoria Regina* with Julie Harris in the role Helen Hayes had originated in the theater. When I asked her how she felt seeing another actress in the part, she said, "I only felt the joy of knowing that it was in such good hands."

Mary Martin and her husband, Richard Halliday, became friends when she did *Born Yesterday* for us in 1956. When I arrived at the studio, someone pointed me out to Mary. She rushed over, threw her arms around me and said, "Mr. Hall, thank you for giving me the chance to play this part. I've always wanted to do it." Later Mary and her husband spent a week with us when she was touring in *Hello, Dolly*. She is all talent. After they left and went to London with the show, Mary made a handsome needlepoint pillow with my initials, signed from "Dick and Mary." I still see Mary now and then. She is the same vivacious person she was the first time I met her.

The "Hall of Fame" continued to be a showcase for some of the world's greatest performers. Katharine Cornell played opposite Charles Boyer in Robert Sherwood's *There Shall Be No Night* in 1957. I also think of Alfred Lunt and Lynn Fontanne in *The Magnificent Yankee*, which won a total of seven awards, five of them Emmys, including best actor, actress and single show. Later Miss Fontanne made a rare appearance, without her husband, as the dowager empress in *Anastasia*. Dame Judith Anderson has been another of the first ladies of the "Hall of Fame," starring in eight productions, three as Lady Macbeth. In 1960 *Macbeth* received six Emmys, including "Program of the Year," and Judith Anderson alone won three Emmys for Hallmark productions in 1954, 1960 and 1961.

It was in 1961 that the National Academy of Television Arts and Sciences presented its first — and only — Emmy ever given to a sponsor. It went to Hallmark for "uplifting the standards of television" — and the citation closed with a memorable comment: "Thank you, Mr. Hall, for caring enough to send the very best in television."

The award gave me a chance to express my gratitude to all the people who helped make it possible. I said, "I want to pay particular tribute to our audience, which has made all of this possible. They have always been understanding through the stumbling years in which we were getting under way in television and through failures and successes. We were always trying — and we are grateful."

In 1969 we took a chance on an original play that many people thought would be too depressing. *Teacher, Teacher* was the poignant story of a mentally retarded boy emerging from his cocoon through the encouragement and inspiration of his tutor. Thirteen-year-old Billy Schulman, who played the role, taught us all something about courage — both in his part and in reality. Billy himself is retarded. It was a chancy piece of casting, and it turned out brilliantly. After the performance,

David McCallum, who played the teacher, and Billy were interviewed on television. Billy proceeded to thank the cast and crew for helping him, which moved McCallum so deeply he broke down and walked away saying, "You're too much."

We took on still another "problem play" the next year with *A Storm in Summer* by Rod Serling. Peter Ustinov played an elderly Jewish proprietor of a delicatessen in Brooklyn, who reluctantly befriends a black child. The boy, acted by N'Gai Dixon, is equally suspicious of this unusual relationship, which ultimately leads to mutual respect and love.

Teacher, Teacher and *A Storm in Summer* brought in more admiring mail than the "Hall of Fame" had ever received before, and the critics were just as enthusiastic. Larry Rummel wrote in the Phoenix Gazette: "*Teacher, Teacher* is an utterly remarkable achievement and television has never been better." The ratings soared along with the awards — five altogether with Emmys for "Outstanding Dramatic Program" and a special one for remarkable little Billy Schulman. *A Storm in Summer* earned Emmys for Peter Ustinov and for best drama and the Christopher Award for the best dramatic special.

This is not to suggest that the "Hall of Fame" never received adverse reaction. One incident I recall occurred during the telecast of *A Bell for Adano* in 1967. A woman called my house, asking for me. She was told that I was watching the show and couldn't come to the phone at the moment. Well, she said, she was watching it, too, and that was why she was calling. I took the phone only to hear her launch into a tirade about the use of the word "damn" in the play, spoken only once. She said she had two teen-aged daughters exposed to this "kind of language" and added that previously she had always felt Hallmark programs were the best on television. Had she ever bothered to call when she liked a show, I asked her? No, she said, but she would in the future. I told her not to bother.

After Donald became president of Hallmark in 1966, he expanded on the initial goals we had set for the "Hall of Fame" to demonstrate that the series could go on to even greater heights. He said: "Properties are chosen for their substance as major dramatic events, and these choices are further guided by the accomplishments of past "Hall of Fame" performances. Every production must also lend diversity to the season in order to give viewers a range of mood as well as important dramatic fare. The

"Hall of Fame" also seeks to inspire and delight. And, finally, we hope that its productions will be permanent contributions to the growth of the television medium as a whole."

The 1970 season was highlighted by a new production of *Hamlet*, starring Richard Chamberlain, who had been so impressive in the role in England. The cast was a director's dream — John Gielgud, Margaret Leighton and Michael Redgrave — and the show was honored with five Emmy awards.

Clarence Peterson in the Chicago Tribune typified the response to *Hamlet*: "The program opened the "Hall of Fame's" twentieth season of sponsoring superior television programs. All too few sponsors care about the quality of the programs they pay for, so long as they gather in vast audiences and offend no one. In gratitude, I think we should all run out and buy a Hallmark card."

A few days later, the National Academy of Television Arts and Sciences held a lunch to honor the "Hall of Fame's" twentieth consecutive season on television. Nancy Hanks, chairman of the National Council on the Arts, spoke on behalf of President Nixon: "In honoring the series, you are paying tribute to television's capacity to reach a broad segment of the American public with performing arts of the highest artistic standards. We believe that the unique longevity of the "Hallmark Hall of Fame" effectively demonstrates that television can make a major contribution to the cultural enrichment of the nation."

By the end of 1978, the "Hall of Fame" had produced 125 shows, outliving any other dramatic program on television. It has won over seventy major awards and honors, including more Emmys than any other program on television. And even our commercials have been cited for their tastefulness and imagination.

The Other World of Winston Churchill

Having succeeded in getting Sir Winston Churchill's paintings for our greeting cards, I was now determined to accomplish two additional goals. More than anything else, I wanted to do a special "Hall of Fame" television show on Sir Winston as an artist. I also felt that the public would greatly benefit by a traveling exhibit of his paintings in this country. But almost everyone who knew him said that he wouldn't be interested. He had never shown his paintings anywhere. On a trip to Chartwell in 1953, I casually approached Sir Winston about the idea. He was definitely against it, feeling that his paintings were not good enough to be exhibited.

Knowing Sir Winston's admiration for President Eisenhower — as a wartime ally, a good friend and a fellow artist — I decided to try for his help in getting Sir Winston's acceptance. The president agreed to write a letter to Churchill and suggested that I deliver it personally. He was also to meet with Prime Minister Harold Macmillan in Bermuda the latter part of March, and he would discuss the exhibit with him. We could hardly have hoped for a greater boost to our efforts.

In June, Sarah Churchill arranged for me to have lunch with Sir Winston at Chartwell. Before leaving for England, I received a copy of the president's letter and a report on his visit with Prime Minister Macmillan. He wrote: "The Prime Minister thinks the exhibition is a splendid idea, as I do. However, he feels that it would be wise not to invite Sir Winston to come with his collection because his strength would probably not permit him to make such a trip without adverse effects and to have to refuse on such ground might be embarrassing to him."

Dr. Franklin Murphy, then chancellor of the University of Kansas and a member of our board of directors, accompanied me to Chartwell. Sir Winston had recently suffered a stroke and was limping slightly and using a cane. But he was fully lucid and spoke only a little hesitantly. Just the same, he invited us to tour the grounds before lunch. As he loved to do, he pointed out the brick wall he had laid. Franklin was so intrigued he walked hurriedly ahead of us to get a good look at it. Franklin was forty-one years old and Sir Winston, eighty-two. When we caught up with him, Sir Winston said, "Don't walk so fast, young man. You're younger than I am. As a matter of fact, it astonishes me that you're the head of a university in America. In England, there's only one fundamental qualification to be a chancellor — you've got to be at least sixty years old. Everything else is secondary."

We raised the question of the exhibit, and he was still lukewarm. After lunch we gave him the letter from President Eisenhower, which he read instantly:

"Dear Winston —

"This note will be delivered to you personally by Joyce Hall and Franklin Murphy, two of my very good friends.

"They will give you the details of a project they have in mind. I send you this letter only to assure you that I join with them in the belief that a traveling exhibition of your paintings in the United States would not only attract a good deal of attention among all the people here interested in painting; but I am certain it would serve in a very definite way to strengthen the friendship between our two countries.

"I am not sure that you realize the tremendous affection that the American people feel for you. It is a very tangible part of the lives of most Americans; in great numbers they would welcome the chance to see your paintings and, in doing so, pay personal tribute to you. The tour would create a wave of good will across our country that would be both exciting and valuable.

"Having said all this, I must also add that, in advance, I enthusiastically support any decision you may make.

"With warm personal regard, and best wishes for your continued health,

"As ever, Ike"

It was apparent the letter made a strong impression on Sir Winston. Still, he was not sold on the idea of parting with his best paintings for an extensive period of time.

Brandy was served, and he explained it was from an old friend in Cognac, France: "Every so often he sends me a keg, and I bottle it here." Then he offered his huge cigars, and Franklin declined. Sir Winston looked over the top of his glasses and said, "Dr. Murphy, I advise you to take a cigar. They are made especially for me from the finest tobacco in Cuba." Franklin replied, "Sir Winston, as you yourself pointed out, I'm a young man, much too young to smoke cigars of this size and strength." Without a moment's hesitation, Sir Winston said, "Dr. Murphy, these cigars are made for boys like you and me." He turned to me and said, "I like your friend Dr. Murphy — even if he is an Irishman."

We still had no answer on the exhibit, but Sir Winston was in a cheerful mood. By late afternoon his personal physician, Lord Moran, joined us for tea. Evidently he made regular visits to check on his famous patient. Sir Winston said to Franklin, "Now Dr. Murphy, let me explain something to you. In England it is a very civilized custom to serve tea in the afternoon, and the custom is to be taken seriously. It gives people a chance to relax late in the day. However, my dear doctor, it is not to be taken *too* seriously. As a matter of fact, I'm going to have Scotch — how about you?" Franklin had Scotch.

By the time we were ready to leave, he had not commented any further on the exhibit. Finally, he said he would think it over. I told him I'd be in London for the rest of the week before sailing. He said he'd have an answer before we left.

In the meantime, Elizabeth, my daughter Barbara and her husband Bob Marshall, had arrived in London. Sarah Churchill invited us to Chartwell to make notes about the paintings that would be of particular interest if her father agreed to the exhibit. In Sir Winston's room, Franklin pointed out a small, impressive bust of Napoleon. Everyone was surprised to see one of England's greatest enemies so honored, but Churchill was fascinated by Napoleon and by French history in general. His favorite figure was Joan of Arc.

On the morning of our departure day, I stopped to see Sir Winston. He was propped up in bed surrounded by papers. His parakeet was flying around the room, occasionally settling on his shoulder, then on a tea cup on his work board. He said he hadn't made up his mind about the exhibit, but if his answer was yes, he would write a letter that I would have by the time I arrived home. If his answer was no, he would cable me aboard ship.

Every time I passed the ship's message room I'd ask if there was anything for me. And finally there was. My heart sank. After all that effort, I figured we'd lost. It was the shortest cable I'd ever received — and the sweetest. It was from Sir Winston's secretary and it said simply, "O.K. Anthony Montague-Brown."

Sir Winston specifically requested that the exhibit be shown at the Smithsonian Institution in Washington and the Metropolitan Museum of Art in New York City. We were already committed to opening the exhibit at the Nelson Gallery of Art in Kansas City. The director of the Chicago Art Institute rejected the exhibit with a public statement about "showing the work of amateurs." But James Rorimer, director of New York's Metropolitan, the nation's greatest museum, said that the exhibit would bring people into museums who weren't in the habit of going. As it turned out, the Metropolitan had the largest crowds in its history to that date. And in spite of the heaviest snow storm in years, the exhibit broke all attendance records at the Nelson Gallery and at almost every museum where it was shown.

I saw Sir Winston several times over the next few years, both at Chartwell and on his visit to the United States in 1959. And in 1960 I attended a showing in London of the "Hallmark Hall of Fame's" production of *Macbeth*, which had been filmed in Scotland. Sir Winston had planned to be there, but he was not well. When I visited him, I was pleased to see how alert he was mentally. Once again he spoke of how much the exhibit of his paintings had meant to him. Later Anthony Montague-Brown expressed it this way: "Sir Winston was grateful for bringing this new adventure into his life at such an advanced age."

On a trip to London in 1962, accompanied by my granddaughter Libby Marshall, I met with Anthony Montague-Brown who had become a good friend. Anthony had served Sir Winston Churchill faithfully for some fourteen years. He had a brilliant war record, having received the Distinguished Flying Cross, and he was a member of the Foreign Office. Sir Winston was in the hospital recovering from a broken leg. I was allowed to have a short visit with him. Libby stayed in the car.

Sir Winston was more confused than I'd ever seen him. Anthony reminded him, "Your friend Ike will be coming to see you to-

The artist, Winston Churchill, at work in 1946

Former President Harry S. Truman and Mr. Hall at a 1958 preview of the Hallmark Sponsored exhibition of paintings by Sir Winston Churchill.

Joyce Hall, Sarah Churchill and Ambassador Averell Harriman at dedication of People-to-People's "Tribute to Sir Winston Churchill" at the New York World's Fair in 1965.

PALLADIAN BRIDGE   WINSTON S. CHURCHILL

A selection of paintings by Sir Winston Churchill as reproduced on Hallmark cards.

Congratulations on Your Anniversary

WINSTON S. CHURCHILL

morrow." For a moment Sir Winston had trouble remembering who Ike was.

He asked if I was alone on the trip, and I told him my granddaughter was with me. "Where is she?" he said — and turned to Anthony with some of the old command in his voice, "Why didn't you bring her up?" Libby had just turned twelve and was shy at that age. I had no idea how she would react. Sir Winston was sitting in a wheelchair smiling and held out his hands to her. She calmly put her hands in his. For about fifteen minutes, Libby and Sir Winston had a much freer conversation than I had had with him. They said goodbye like old friends. He was eighty-seven that summer, and I wondered if I'd ever see him again.

Sir Winston's health continued to decline, although he doggedly held on — and now and then he'd have a great resurgence of strength. I was in London in July of 1964 with Duane Bogie from our agency, Foote, Cone & Belding, and David Strout, director of the Hallmark Gallery in New York. We had a number of things to accomplish, but most of all I wanted to see Sir Winston.

One of our assignments was to gather materials for a Churchill exhibit at the Hallmark Gallery. And we were still determined to do a television special on some aspect of Sir Winston's life. These projects were to coincide as a tribute to the man on his ninetieth birthday — November 30, 1964. But there were options on just about everything Sir Winston had ever written. Finally we learned that a small volume by him was available — *Painting as a Pastime*.

In the book he explained how he had turned to painting after being dismissed as First Lord of the Admiralty. He was out of favor in his own country and branded a warmonger for his urgent warnings of Hitler's intentions. "It was then that the muse of painting came to my rescue," he wrote. "Happy are the painters, for they shall not be lonely. Light and colour, peace and hope, will keep them company to the end of the day."

Jack LeVien, who had produced two programs based on Churchill's memoirs, was the perfect choice to produce the "Hallmark Hall of Fame" show, *The Other World of Winston Churchill*. It was telecast on his ninetieth birthday the same day in the United States, England and the Commonwealth countries. We made the hour-long color documentary available to schools throughout the world.

The Churchill exhibit at the Hallmark Gallery also opened on his ninetieth birthday. Dave Strout described it as "an intimate study of a monumental figure whose public life spanned the reigns of six sovereigns — from Victoria to the second Elizabeth." It was a remarkable collection of art and memorabilia from Sir Winston's public and family life, including his paintings, first editions of his books, family heirlooms, portraits and sculptures.

The New York World's Fair opened that year, too, and for our People to People exhibit we were loaned more than forty Churchill paintings by his family, friends and even the British royal family. The great Oscar Nemon bust was exhibited as well as a sculpture Sir Winston did of Nemon. There were a number of historic documents, including a draft of the Atlantic Charter. And perhaps the highlight of the exhibit was an authentic reconstruction of Sir Winston's study at Chartwell.

The 1964 trip was the last time I was to see Sir Winston. He had just returned from the House of Commons where he had been singularly honored in a manner that was perhaps unprecedented in English history. When I arrived at his Hyde Park home, he was sitting in the library leaning on a cane. He seemed to remember old times but was terribly weary. I soon excused myself and joined Anthony in an anteroom where I could still look in on Sir Winston. In a few minutes Lady Churchill entered the library. She approached him from behind, gently put her hands on his shoulders, leaned over and kissed him on top of his head.

It was the last sight I had of Sir Winston Churchill. I try to forget. I try to remember the robust figure who bounded into the living room that noon at Chartwell when I met him for the first time. And I can.

The Vapors of Past Experience

Several years ago, Richard Deems, chairman of Hearst's Magazines Division, was visiting us. We were discussing a meeting I'd had that day, and I expressed concern that our people weren't sure our objectives were attainable. I felt that if they just believed they could be accomplished — they would be. But for some reason people resist new ideas.

Dick said this was a common experience in publishing as well. He had a drawing in his office of the Wright Brothers' plane Kitty Hawk. It showed the figure of a man talking to Orville Wright — with the caption: "It won't fly, Orville."

That seemed to sum up the whole problem to me. With Dick's permission I had some tent cards printed with this message. I kept one on my desk for many years. When anyone told me something couldn't be done, I pointed to the card. I had been trying to say the same thing in many more words all my life.

It reminded me of a statement by General David Sarnoff, the dynamic founder of RCA who was a wizard in electronics. At the dedication of a new science building at Princeton University, he said: "Any intelligent man who has watched color television and has seen a jet plane take off would have to believe that anything the mind of man can conceive can be accomplished."

On another occasion, talking with Dr. Norman Vincent Peale, he turned to me and asked, "What is the biggest problem you have in your organization?" I said, "Selling ideas." Now, Dr. Peale is one of our most successful ministers and writers, and he replied wearily, "My job is selling, too, and I just have to keep working at it all the time."

And I recall President Eisenhower saying that his greatest problem was selling ideas — to his staff, to his cabinet, to Congress and, ultimately, to the American people. Winston Churchill was one of the greatest salesmen who ever lived. He sold the free world on arming itself, probably the most important selling job ever accomplished.

Selling ideas is the most crucial of all jobs. Essentially it is getting people to think your way. In that sense, I've been selling all my life.

Early in our business, I learned that the best way to keep track of changing tastes and trends was to spend time in good retail stores every chance I got. I'd go to California each spring and New York in the fall just looking for new ideas. Right after Thanksgiving, New York's great stores are full of new and exciting merchandise. I found that browsing, or what I call "professional shopping" — whether I bought anything or not — was a great source of ideas. I'd make notes on three by five cards, which I always have with me.

On one trip, walking on Fifth Avenue, I saw a dress with a beautiful and unusual pattern in a store window. I bought it for Elizabeth, but I also wanted to see if it would influence our people. We made dozens of adaptations of the pattern for greeting cards, party goods and gift wrappings.

One of the most successful gift wrappings was inspired by a cosmetic jar made of frosted glass with an iridescent floral pattern. The jar cost ten dollars, but it was worth ten thousand dollars in ideas. On another trip I saw *My Fair Lady* and was charmed by the costumes and set decorations. I contacted the show's designer, Cecil Beaton, and had him develop a group of Christmas cards based on his work.

I returned from these trips with a multitude of ideas — and purchases. It could be anything from a piece of sculpture to a doll to a restaurant menu. Then I'd call small groups of our designers together to discuss how they might apply these items to our products. I'd say what I had in mind, then ask them to try to think of something better.

The constant search for ideas is what makes the greeting card business so fascinating. I've always told our people that they could get ideas anywhere — riding a bus, taking a walk, looking in windows, reading a magazine, talking to people. I wasn't saying they should copy someone else's ideas, but use them for inspiration for new designs and to improve existing ones.

I also said that they should never overlook the obvious. The thing that's right under your nose is often the best. Some time ago we had our artists doing sketches for greeting cards following the exact details of photographs. They worked so well that it finally occurred to us to use the photographs themselves. Could anything be more obvious? Yet these were the first color photographs used on greeting cards.

The point is that you never know when a good idea will pop up. I've found the best times to think were sitting by the fire in the evening and shaving in the morning. After reading a newspaper story about jelly beans, I thought they would make an interesting gift wrapping, arranged in a colorful pattern. It became a long-time favorite.

Our retail stores have always been a source of new ideas. To do the right kind of job as a manufacturer, you can never lose touch with the retailer and the consumer. A manufacturer must have a retailer's outlook. That is why we have always been in the retail business.

I've learned as much from our retail stores as I ever have from scientific research. In fact, the stores have always provided the raw material we use in researching public tastes and buying habits. Research, as we know it today, wasn't even used by large companies until about 1920. My experience in this area started in 1918, before it even had a name. We have been told that we were one of the first manufacturers to use market research in business.

Back then, we wanted to know why some of our greeting cards sold ten times better than others. We put a carefully-worked-out system in one of our first stores that told us how many cards we had sold of each type every month. We kept the display full so the record would be as meaningful as possible. We haven't changed this system much since then. Now, of course, our information is from many stores and a computer tabulates the results.

People often ask me how we arrive at the right decisions in a business as complicated as ours. There just aren't any pat rules for making decisions. Alfred Frankfurter, who was a friend and an art critic, gave the best answer I've ever heard. When he was asked how he judged a painting, he first stumbled through a long explanation about color, composition and lighting. Then he paused and said firmly, "No, what I really do is use the vapors of past experience." He didn't have to analyze a painting piece by piece. He could look at it and let his mental computer add up the minuses and pluses.

The creative process in making decisions is simply "the vapors of past experience." When someone shows me a greeting card I don't like, I generally know exactly why, but sometimes have a hard time explaining it. It's just something that's accumulated over the years.

I've been accused of running a one-man show — perhaps because I don't particularly believe in running a business by meetings and committees. More often they just complicate the decision-making process. I'm a firm believer in the idea that there is a simpler and better way to do almost anything.

I've always disliked meetings — and I never meet anyone who says he likes them. The executives I talk to tell me meetings usually are a waste of time. But they must mean everyone else's meetings because they keep having them. Of course, some meetings are necessary. But if there were fewer of them with less people in half as much time, the results would be just as good — if not a whole lot better.

And I've never heard of a committee solving a really important problem. The old adage that "a camel is a horse designed by a committee" is all too true. I remember sculptor Oscar Nemon taking me to guildhall in London to see a statue he had done of Winston Churchill. I was disappointed because it wasn't nearly as good as the one he had done for Queen Elizabeth. I frankly asked him why one was so much better than the other. He replied that the bust at guildhall had been done to please a committee of liverymen who had commissioned it, while the other had been done to please one person, the queen.

Still, the most productive business procedure I know of is simply to work long and hard. I've never known anyone who got anywhere who didn't work his nails off. Hard work is unusual today — and it gets unusual results.

But maybe there's always been a shortage of hard workers. I have a photocopy of a letter from Abraham Lincoln that he wrote at the request of a friend who had two sons seeking employment: "The lady — bearer of this — says she has two sons who want to work — Set them at it, if possible — Wanting to work is so rare an event it should be encouraged."

When my children were in school, I was never as concerned about the grades they got as I was about how hard they worked to get them. I preferred to see a child of mine get a "B" — really worked for — than an easy "A." Tough, competitive work is a great source of tension, which some people today consider bad for an individual. But tension is what makes people alert. When they just go placidly along, it's like floating downstream in a boat. They are lulled to sleep. But when things get rough, people have to be on their toes all the time.

To stay alert, one of the most important things a man can do is assess himself and his work on a regular basis. Somehow I started doing this

As the corporation grew, employees joined in making a special Christmas greeting for "Mr. J.C." These took the form of large format cards and the Christmas "card" trees.

every New Year's. I'd think about what was wrong with the way I was operating and what I should do about it. Once a year isn't often enough to do this — but it's a lot better than never.

If a man goes into business only with the idea of making a lot of money, chances are he won't. But if he puts service and quality first, the money will take care of itself. Producing a first-class product that is a real need is a much stronger motivation for success than getting rich.

If a man runs a hotel as well as Hernando Courtright ran the Beverly Hills Hotel, he'll make money. If he runs a magazine as well as DeWitt Wallace and Lila Acheson Wallace ran the *Reader's Digest,* he'll make money. If he runs a store as well as Marshall Field did, he'll make money. But more importantly, he'll make a real contribution to society.

Among the "unsophisticated arts" (a phrase I first heard from designer Charles Eames), quality retailing has to be close on the top. It has a tremendous effect on the community and its culture. "Clothes and custom mold the mind," Confucius said 2,500 years ago — and it is still true today.

Not long ago I read an outstanding book on retailing, *The Great Shops of Europe,* by Jerome Klein. Its illustrations and typography reflected the book's quality. In his introduction, the author stated: "Surely the great shops of any city or village are a lucid reflection of a nation's culture . . . . In some respects, a nation's great shops are as important as its museums. Museums gather the rarities of many cultures and eras. Great shops reflect a people's artful skills and the modes and manners of a particular time."

Neiman-Marcus in Dallas played a major role in changing a crossroads shopping community into one of the finest quality markets in the country. The Bullock's and Magnin stores turned the pioneer market of southern California into one of the most delightful shopping areas in the world. They took the lead in influencing people to dress casually — and in good style — and set the pace for the entire country. New York has more than its share of great stores — Bonwit Teller, Bergdorf's, Sak's Fifth Avenue, Lord & Taylor, Bloomingdale's — and, yes, Macy's and Gimbels. They are tourist attractions in themselves.

Modern merchandising has changed shopping into an adventure rather than just a chore. To realize its effect on the public, just stand in a

240

fine store that handles a variety of merchandise and watch people's faces as they see things that please them.

I became familiar with the importance of quality retailing early in life, working in two bookstores in Nebraska when I was in my teens. One store offered exceptional merchandise for a small town, and the other's was poorly displayed and poorly stocked. It had a huge supply of what I call bric-a-brac — things that had been around a long time that the owner should have thrown out. From this store I learned what didn't sell, and from the other I learned the importance of quality.

Picture post cards had come into their own, and we had a good display of them in the front of the store. It turned a losing operation into one that made a small profit. They not only sold well, but brought people into the store who would then buy other things. I got a kick out of post cards. It was fun to sell them, fun to buy them and fun to send them.

Being new, post cards attracted a transient type of manufacturer out to make a fast buck. He believed that if he underpriced the other fellow, he would get the business. Soon European and American manufacturers began making cheaper post cards. And the cheaper they got, the poorer they sold. Finally people quit buying post cards. For about ten years, I saw the post card business die a slow death. Then I concluded that there was a quality business and a cheap business — and I preferred quality.

In the early days of greeting cards, it was generally believed that you could make quality cards for a limited volume or cheap cards for a large volume. I never accepted this idea. I felt that the larger your business became, the more you could afford to bring in outstanding talent and equipment to make the finest cards.

As the industry grew and the public became exposed to better cards, tastes began to change. Retailers soon realized that the amount of paper in a greeting card didn't determine its value any more than the amount of fabric does in a dress. Stores that sold large, cheaply-made cards at lower prices stopped handling them because the public rejected them. Manufacturers of these cards either had to start making better ones or go out of business. Many who tried to improve the quality of their cards simply didn't know how.

We always kept in mind that greeting cards were also a social custom. More than almost any other product, a greeting card not only reflects the taste of the buyer, it also makes a judgment about the taste of the recipient. The various factors that make other products appealing do not

241

always apply to greeting cards. Most products are for self-consumption. When you look at *them*, you don't have to think about how your friend in Denver would react to them. You do with greeting cards.

It's been my job over half a century to pay close attention to public tastes and trends. When we were first in business, taste improved slowly. But as better transportation and communication facilities developed, it stepped up. Public taste had a noticeable boost during World War I as a result of greater exposure to the world in general. And after World War II, this was even more apparent. Today it is a computer job to keep up with the space-age speed of improving tastes and changing trends.

Richard Gump, whose San Francisco store carried products of the finest craftsmanship from around the world, wrote a book called *Good Taste Costs No More*. It impressed me, and I wrote to tell him so. A short time later he came to Kansas City, and we had several meetings discussing good taste as it applied to our products.

After his visit, he sent me a letter opener and a magnifying glass with handles made of two parts of a heavy jade belt buckle from a Chinese ceremonial robe. They have been on my desk ever since as a constant reminder of the importance of taste and quality in making greeting cards.

People confuse taste and quality. Taste is temporary, quality is permanent. Broad lapels and wide ties are approved taste today. But forty years ago they were what gangsters wore in movies; thirty years ago they were "zoot suits;" ten years ago they were daring. Today, of course, they're very smart. In another five years they'll be old-fashioned; in ten years they'll be ridiculous; in thirty years they'll be quaint. And in fifty years they'll be back in style.

It troubles me that there's a great compromise with quality in America today. This has affected us adversely in all walks of life — in the education of our children, the conduct of our government, the manufacture of our automobiles, the design of our houses and commercial buildings — and even in the movies we see and the television we watch. There has been an increase in shoddy craftsmanship in America and less pride among the repair trades. Public services have declined. Deliveries arrive late or damaged — and often the wrong item is sent.

Is it any wonder that the consumerism movement has become a great force in this country? It may be too critical at times, but more often it's right. Its success has clearly demonstrated a need. And manufacturers and retailers should take it seriously and apply it constructively. When the consumer speaks, we'd better listen.

In part, our rapidly changing times have brought about this compromise with quality. Things have moved too fast for people to change them. No wonder young people are baffled and looking for different answers — and hopefully better ones. But, too often, they find worse ones.

Another factor that has encouraged the compromise with quality is the increase in mergers and conglomerates. There haven't been too many organizations combining forces to improve quality. Some of them do, but the ones I hear about are those that only want power and profit.

In the bookstore in Nebraska many years ago, I used to open shipping crates from Japan containing all sorts of paper lanterns, paper flags, jumping jacks and stuffed chicks. These novelties were popular, and we sold a good many of them. In those days the United States didn't take Japan seriously as a competitor in world markets or even American markets. Japan had a reputation for making sleazy goods, while the great new crop of American industrial giants were turning out automobiles and furniture as fast as they once made matches. And, more significantly, they were taking pride in making them.

But somehow Japan discovered the magic word quality. And today a large percentage of fine cameras that come to this country are Japanese. The same is true of a variety of electronic devices, motorcycles and even automobiles. They also go to countries where we compete with the same products. As a result we're losing the very markets that made us great — and losing them fast.

It is hard for us to compete in price with American labor costs so high. Quality has to be the answer. It's not going to be easy to change this trend — and it's not going to change unless we change.

We need some contemporary DaVincis, Chippendales, Wrens, Edisons, Einsteins and Franklins, men like the late Charles Eames and Henry Dreyfuss. In a real sense, we have them and always will because we have their creative achievements as a guide toward greater quality.

There is not only more need, but more opportunity today for better draftsmen, legislators, educators, television and products and services of all kinds. We have the new technology to build on. It shouldn't make us lazier or less inventive. It should be a boon to creativity. And up to the point we are willing to pursue it, it can release us for more time to improve the quality of our endeavors and our lives.

It will take great courage and enthusiasm. America can furnish all of this and more. We will, if we care enough.

J.C. Hall

EPILOGUE/
APPENDIX

The Pursuit of Excellence

These informal reminiscences were never intended to be memoirs in any exacting sense. Joyce C. Hall simply began to review the accumulation of personal correspondence, memorandums, speeches and notes he'd written over the years. The most persistent theme that emerged was a care and concern for the quality of Hallmark products.

That Hallmark would become the massive worldwide operation it is today never for a moment occurred to Hall in those early, lonely years when he set up business in a cramped little room in Kansas City's Y.M.C.A. Nor did Joyce Hall envision himself becoming the architect of an industry. In the course of building a business, it simply followed that he, more than anyone else, popularized the greeting card custom in the world.

Not long ago, in general conversation with Hall, he was asked just what were the toughest decisions he ever had to make. After a few moments thought, he began jotting down a list in his firm, legible script. He first cited the move to Kansas City in 1910, having to leave his family and a secure job working with his brothers in a retail store.

The list continued: To turn down a large order for cards at a reduced price, an order that would have doubled his volume at a time when the company was still struggling — he refused to give the discount on the basis that all his customers had to be treated alike; to build the company's first plant; to create fixtures for displaying greeting cards; to institute an automatic reorder system for dealers; to go into national advertising; to call the cards Hallmark and later to change the name of the company from Hall Brothers to Hallmark; to buy the properties adjacent to the main headquarters; and to diversify the company's product lines. These decisions were often made alone, against considerable opposition.

In still another way, Hall's decision list serves as a rundown on the company's many innovations in the greeting card industry. The introduction of display fixtures with a built-in reorder system literally revolutionized the industry. The system came about after years of studying records on the retail sale of cards. Initially, Hall depended on his memory of what sold well and what did not. Eventually he developed written records. Later an automatic reorder system was created.

Utilizing one of the most sophisticated computer operations in private industry, Hallmark experts know the exact selection of cards for each suburb, a different selection for downtowns and yet another for changing neighborhoods. In fact, every one of the independent retail outlets has a group of Hallmark products scientifically picked for its location.

Daily sales reports running into the millions of items indicate whether puppies outsell kittens, how lilacs fare against roses and whether get-well cards still sell faster in Atlanta than they do in Pittsburgh. Successes or failures are spotted instantly.

The idea for this highly refined research largely stems from another of Hall's principles. Quite simply he believes that a manufacturer has to understand merchandising on a retail level to be successful. And how better to judge the market place than to have a store of your own? From the beginning, the stores Hallmark established served as a basis for the company's research long before the word "research" came into the vocabulary. Today, those stores are scattered across the country yet number only a dozen or so. Joyce Hall believed a supplier should never be in serious competition with his customers.

Going into national advertising was generally regarded as "Hall's Folly." How can you advertise a product without a name? A customer can instantly identify a bar of soap he's seen advertised, but not a greeting card with the manufacturer's name hidden on the back. The results are history; the name Hallmark is synonymous with greeting cards.

The "Hallmark Hall of Fame" launched the most distinguished and enduring dramatic series in television history. It has been heaped with more honors and awards than any other show on television. Hallmark had rejected, against everyone's well-meant advice, the popular game and quiz shows, crime and variety programs, westerns and domestic comedies. The stunning result was that Shakespeare, original plays and

Broadway successes were brought to television in prime time.

The vast diversification of Hallmark has largely been directed by Hall's son, Donald, including the development of Crown Center, the eighty-five-acre complex that is a self-contained commercial and residential community.

Don Hall is a modest chief executive officer unlikely to repeat the strong one-man rule of his father. He has surrounded himself with a gifted management team made up of veteran Hallmark employees up from the ranks as well as selected outsiders who have brought the specialized skills needed by the company in its rapid growth.

It is not unusual that the selected reminiscences of Joyce Hall say so little about the last fifteen years of the corporation's history. To men like Joyce Hall, the real excitement has always been in the effort, in the struggle. Success is not something to be enjoyed in itself, but rather a justification of the struggle and the risk of the early years.

Let us look, then, in these closing pages, at some of the events and characteristics of Hallmark Cards under the influence and guidance of Don Hall. The period of time covers approximately the two decades of the 1960s and the 1970s. This is not to suggest that the leadership of the founder was not present during this time. Joyce Hall was president and chairman of the board until March of 1966. Long after the presidency of his son, the chairman was a towering figure in the corporation's daily business. However, the presidency of Donald J. Hall, who became chief executive officer in 1966, is a most fitting subject for the epilogue to his father's book.

Every new direction Hallmark takes is cautiously examined against what the company knows it does best. This attitude has prevailed since Hallmark's first departure from greeting cards back in the 1920's when Hall and his brother, Rollie, introduced decorative gift wrapping paper in this country. In the late fifties, Hallmark recognized that party decorations were limited and, for the most part, rather drab. Soon a line of paper party products was sampled with instant success. These were followed shortly by playing cards as a companion product.

Hallmark does not think of a new product as a commodity as much as a social custom. And it became apparent at Hallmark that the most effective way to be of total service to its dealers was to establish complete

This Hallmark Distribution Center, close to Interstate 35 and the Kansas City International Airport, is situated on a thirty-eight-acre site near Liberty, Missouri.

The heart of the operation is a computer which directs merchandise onto conveyor belts and automatic cranes which send it to any of 163,000 storage bins. The computer also keeps track of customer orders which are filled by hand from racks containing thousands of different products.

The computer refills the racks as needed, prints self-adhering shipping labels, and further directs the goods toward their retail destination.

Outbound to customers, thirty cartons a minute whiz by one of three sorting stations, (below), where an operator reads a code number and sends each carton to one of 596 "accumulating lines." Immediately thereafter, multicarton orders go to the loading docks for shipment to the retailers.

"social expression" shops in the largest and finest stores in the country. Social stationery was added to an established line of thank-you notes in 1963. It was soon followed by calendars and keepsake albums.

Intensive nationwide research was done on the salability of gift books, developing over one hundred titles and testing the response to them. When the results were in, Hallmark began publishing books in 1966 based on the themes the public liked best. They ranged from *Sonnets from the Portuguese* to *A Treasury of Mark Twain*, from *The Poems of Doctor Zhivago* to *Aesop's Fables*. They also include children's books featuring three-dimensional pop-up illustrations. A number of Hallmark books have now passed the half-million mark in sales.

In 1967, Hallmark bought Springbok Editions, a company that manufactured quality jigsaw puzzles. The puzzles were mainly reproductions of fine paintings by such artists as Jackson Pollack, Miro, Picasso and Dali. Springbok became an integral part of Hallmark with a greatly expanded line of puzzles, some in circular and octagonal shapes. Posters, plaques and a variety of other items were added to this line of leisure products.

There was one prominent omission in the company's party goods — candles. Beautifully decorative candles were being produced in Germany and Austria, and Hallmark felt that people would buy them here if the design and quality were the finest. So fashion colors were introduced to candles in a variety of decorative designs. In two or three years, Hallmark became the leading manufacturer of candles for home use.

A natural outgrowth of the stationery line was writing instruments. But the Halls wanted them to be distinguished from well-established lines of pens and pencils. More than 250 laboratory tests were made to perfect processes and parts, and by 1970 an elegant line of writing instruments was put on the market. Their unique feature was the use of wood casings — walnut, rosewood, wenge, cordia, teak and tulipwood — which immediately set them apart from the standard lines.

Hallmark attributes much of its stunning growth to a basic management philosophy — that the company's success is in direct ratio to its dealers' success. Hallmark supports these dealers with a dizzying variety of services, ranging far beyond national advertising and the quality of the products themselves.

The bond between Hallmark and the retail outlets that market the firm's products has been steadily strengthened through the years. Store planning services, retail training classes, advanced retail seminars and guidance on taxes and insurance are among the extraordinary services that Hallmark extends to the retailers who offer the company's products to the general public. In addition, the company offers counseling services on every element at the point of sale, maintaining constant personal contact with its dealers. Nearly a thousand persons are involved in the firm's marketing and marketing services area, a graphic example of progress over the days when Joyce Hall struggled alone to install a four-foot fixture in a single store.

Shortly after becoming chief executive officer, Don Hall initiated a vast building program, including the addition of one million square feet of space to the company's international headquarters. The Hallmark complex now contains more than two million square feet of space, nearly twice that of the Empire State Building.

Expansion programs for virtually every Hallmark installation were undertaken. A huge distribution center, estimated to be the third largest structure in the nation as measured by cubic footage, was built in nearby Liberty, Missouri. Designed and developed by Hallmark engineers, its combination of computer and mechanical operation was a prototype since emulated across the nation. A companion structure has since been announced for Enfield, Connecticut, already the home of the firm's distribution for the Eastern seaboard.

Similarly, the early manufacturing plants in Lawrence, Leavenworth and Topeka, Kansas, were either replaced or remodeled and enlarged after 1966. Today, the production capacity of Hallmark Cards is housed in vast modern centers, any one of which would dwarf the fondest dream of the elder Hall during his fledgling years.

One of Don Hall's early moves in becoming president was to emphasize Hallmark International. Prior to 1958, the company had only distributed its products in this country and Canada with a few exports to England and Latin America. Today, the company distributes in all of North America, Europe and Australia as well as sections of South America, Asia and Africa. And new manufacturing plants have been built in Toronto, Canada, and Dublin, Ireland.

Travelers now encounter the Hallmark brand name in more than one hundred countries with greetings appearing in twenty languages ranging from the common European languages to Thai, Japanese, Tagalog, Arabic and Greek.

San Francisco Tower Condominium

Health Club at Crown Center West

Aerial view of Crown Center, summer 1979

Crown Center West Appartments

In 1959, Hallmark International made its first major move overseas, opening extensive operations in the British Isles. Until then, Christmas cards had been the only greeting cards sold there. People have often asked the Halls about the difference in taste between the United States and England. Will the same cards sell in both countries? Don Hall believes the answer is yes. Except for the different holidays in various countries, he feels sentiment and even humor can be translated and used anywhere with about the same relative success.

One of the most unusual programs Don Hall introduced during the 1960s was the Hallmark Training Center for people unqualified for jobs under standard criteria. He located the center amid these "unemployables," thereby making it easier for them to get to work and to start a new life. Upon acceptance into the program, trainees are compensated as any other new employee. Once skilled or semi-skilled in a useful Hallmark operation, the men and women are transferred into normal operations at one of the Hallmark production centers. The Halls refused federal funding for the concept and are convinced the Training Center is beneficial to both the company and the community.

The company that Joyce Hall turned over to his only son in 1966 today bears less the mark of the patriarch than the modern management techniques of Don Hall. The struggle of the early years, so personally sketched in the first sections of this book, are gone; the firm is an unqualified success, one of the proud flagships of the free enterprise tradition.

But Joyce Hall's legacy to his son and to Don Hall's modern organization is everywhere apparent in any Hallmark location. "I'm hell bent on quality," Joyce Hall used to say. He is, and it shows. The sourdough bread in the employee cafeteria must still pass his muster. The Hallmark Gallery on Fifth Avenue in New York City must meet his tough standards, as must the firm's locations at Disneyland and Disney World. Don Hall shows no inkling of debasing this quality currency in either product, people or practices.

As the corporation has expanded under its new leadership, it has acquired subsidiaries much like itself. The 1976 purchase of Trifari, Krussman and Fishel, Inc., producers of Jewels by Trifari, a quality costume jewelry concern, is typical. Trifari was family-owned, privately held and much concerned about the well-being of its employees and the quality control of its product. When the three families chose to sell, they would sell only to Hallmark.

The same experience was repeated three years later with the acquisition of the Charles D. Burnes Company of Boston, manufacturers of photographic frames. Owned by the Gordon family, privately held, the firm's sentiments regarding the sale were expressed by Samuel Gordon, the senior member: "When it is advantageous to sell a family business, you sell only to quality. We have done this by selecting Hallmark. They will maintain our traditions, because they have similar attitudes toward ethics and high standards. Their concern for their employees and customers is remarkably similar to the philosophies of the Gordon family."

For all its size and varied complexities, Don Hall directs Hallmark with an open-door policy that is the antithesis of most large corporations. He is readily accessible to his professional managers and division directors. Decision making can be immediate, avoiding the layered red tape that encumbers so many firms. The producers of network television specials like to present "Hallmark Hall of Fame" ideas to Hallmark because the decision is forthcoming in hours, not weeks.

It is the management team at Hallmark of which Don Hall is most proud. It has given the company a new direction and new vitality while preserving historic values. Crown Center, for example, is personally guided by Don Hall, but he is quick to credit the expertise of his own staff plus the noted architecture of Edward Larrabee Barnes, Harry Weese and Norman Fletcher, among others. Whether one calls it a pursuit of excellence, or quality — his father's term — Don Hall has set the highest possible standards for Crown Center. Devoted to his native Kansas City, he expects the $500 million project to substantially boost the community. He would also like to contribute to the progress of all center cities by this example of what one company can do in redevelopment, without using public funds. And, finally, there is the concern for aesthetics and the general public. While attending activities within the Crown Center complex such as ethnic festivals, music, exhibits and sports, people walk past museum-quality sculpture by Alexander Calder and David Smith.

Crown Center is the largest and most recent evidence of the impact Hallmark success has had on the Kansas City community. This is hardly accidental. For nearly seventy years, the Hall family has had the desire that corporate success would relate directly to the progress of the headquarters community. Everything the corporation does is done with the hope that some benefit will accrue to the city, to its economic strength, and to the quality of life of its citizens. Good jobs for local people were a primary concern during the building years; today, leadership projects are more tangible, more visible. Whatever the era, Joyce and Don Hall always intended that Hallmark Cards, Inc. be a positive impact on Kansas City and Kansas Citians.

From its electronic data processing capability to the architecture of Crown Center, Hallmark has a modernity that fits the forward thinking management concepts of Don Hall and his colleagues. Yet, the firm remains a blend of yesteryear's virtues, today's technology and tomorrow's fashion and design trends. It is "socially responsible," to use the term applied to private business and its role in society. But Don Hall insists on something called Social Responsibility Plus, a program that decrees the corporation do more than is expected of it, more than mere compliance. It has taken the firm into urban redevelopment (Crown Center), a creative art program for elementary school children (Kaleidoscope), and the training of normally unqualified workers (the Hallmark Training Center).

What is happening at Hallmark today pleases Joyce Clyde Hall. It goes without saying that he is immensely proud of his son and what is being accomplished at the company. He is also astonished at some of the financial figures he reads, ranging from the firm's annual sales to the cost of the new 750-room Hyatt Regency being built by Hallmark in Crown Center. But Joyce Hall knows figures are relative to the times. He remains most interested in the unchanging value of quality and uncompromising business ethics. It is these areas that he watches most closely.

As the editing of these reminiscenses came to a close, Joyce Hall reflected at length, then summarized his thoughts, saying, "A business doesn't grow up like a mushroom — it needs to be helped." He was thinking about the focus of his book, the concentration of material about himself and he was worried about the lack of recognition of his immediate family and thousands of dedicated employees. Throughout his life he has gloried in the active support of his wife and children in the family business, proud of their involvement and thankful for the contributions of each. Likewise, he wishes there were some way to recognize in this volume the employees who helped the "mushroom" grow. He is ever cognizant of their importance.

Joyce and Donald Hall have had an "unusual father and son relationship" as one veteran Kansas City businessman put it. Few father-son teams have made such a smooth, positive and constructive transition in running a business as large and progressive as Hallmark Cards, Inc. The younger man is surely Joyce Hall's living legacy, a son who has preserved the finest intangibles created by the first generation and enhanced them in the changing and growing physical environment of modern business.

This devotion to quality, this pursuit of excellence has always been the essence of Joyce Hall's philosophy. It is gratifying to him that the same devotion has been transferred to his son. But Joyce Hall's greatest satisfaction surely comes from the secure knowledge that his idea of quality is shared by the employees of the family firm, and, through them, to millions of people who exchange Hallmark cards and Hallmark gifts throughout the world.

Personal and Corporate Chronology

1891 Joyce Hall born August 29. Third son of George Nelson Hall and Nancy Dudley Houston Hall.

1900 Joyce Hall sells door-to-door for California Perfume Company (company later renamed Avon Products).

1902 Brothers Rollie B. Hall and William F. Hall buy bookstore in Norfolk, Nebraska, and Hall family moves to Norfolk.

1903 Joyce Hall accompanies brother Rollie on Rollie's candy sales trip through Nebraska, Wyoming and Black Hills of South Dakota — making part of the trip on the fabled Deadwood Stage.

1905 Hall brothers begin wholesaling post cards as the Norfolk Postcard Company.

1910 Joyce Clyde Hall (middle name now selected by Rollie) moves to Kansas City, Missouri, to expand post card wholesaling business. He operates the business from his YMCA room.

YMCA complains about large mail volume, so J.C. rents a room on the third floor of the nearby Braley Building, 308 East 10th Street.

1911 Rollie, Marie (J.C.'s younger sister) and Mrs. Hall join Joyce in Kansas City, occupying a house at Troost and Manheim Road.

Company moves to 915 Broadway.

1912 Popularity (and quality) of post cards declining. Greeting cards added to business.

1913 Growth of business requires greater space. Company moves to Corn Belt Bank Building, 1019 Grand Avenue.

1914 Retail display area with cards and stationery opens in Corn Belt Bank Building.

Become publishers with twenty engraved Christmas cards.

1915 Hall Brothers office burns — including entire inventory — leaving company $17,000 in the red, and all Valentine orders unfilled.

Company moves (all that remains of it is a safe) to second floor of Starr Piano Company, 1025 Grand Avenue.

Hall Brothers purchases engraving presses and begins manufacturing some of their own cards.

1916 Nancy Dudley Houston Hall dies at the age of forty-six.

A retail store opens at 113 East 11th.

1919 Company growth initiates move to 1114 Grand Avenue.

Charles S. Stevenson joins Hall Brothers.

Introduce cards simply expressing friendship.

Expand sales to East Coast and West Coast.

1920 W.F. Hall joins the business.

1921 Joyce Clyde Hall marries Elizabeth Ann Dilday.

1922 Salesmen are now covering all forty-eight states.

Elizabeth Ann Hall born on July 8.

Decorative gift wrap introduced in the retail store on Petticoat Lane.

1923 Company moves to a new building at an employee-selected site at 26th and Walnut.

Barbara Louise Hall born October 21.

	Company opens an employee cafeteria.
1925	First offer to merge — from Eaton, Crane and Pike — is received. Offer declined.
	Art staff now numbers twelve.
1926	"Flat cards" — heavy, laminated, non-folding cards — are introduced.
	Phenomenal flop: "Greetaphones."
1927	Joyce and Elizabeth Hall purchase house and forty-one acres at 103rd and State Line.
1928	Donald Joyce Hall born July 9.
	Begin using Hallmark on the back of every card.
	First national ad (written by J.C. Hall) appears in *Ladies Home Journal*.
1932	"Wunderflowers" are another setback.
	Begin using Walt Disney characters on cards.
1935	Joyce Hall purchases dairy herd.
1936	William P. Harsh joins company.
	Headquarters relocated to 25th and Grand Avenue.
	New attractive display fixtures that revolutionize the greeting card industry are introduced to stores, using converted travel trailers as conveyances.
1938	"Tony Wons' Radio Scrapbook" airs on WMAQ in Chicago to test the idea of radio advertising.
1940	Wons' show moves to network radio.
1942	Hallmark-sponsored "Meet Your Navy" presented on network radio.
1944	First use of "When You Care Enough to Send the Very Best."
	Foote, Cone & Belding, of Chicago, is engaged as the company's advertising agency.
1945	Hall Brothers opens a plant in Topeka, Kansas.
1946	Market research program starts.
	"Radio *Readers' Digest*" airs on network radio.
1947	Hall Brothers begins manufacturing in Leavenworth, Kansas.
1948	Storybook Dolls cards are introduced.
	First international Hallmark Art Award Competition is held.
1949	Hallmark-and-Crown becomes a registered trademark.
1950	Halls Store opens at 1114 Grand Avenue.
	Joyce Hall begins long association with Dwight Eisenhower.
	Twelve Winston Churchill paintings appear on Christmas cards.
1959	Ambassador Cards is launched to serve large, mass-marketing stores.
	Lawrence, Kansas, plant opens.
	Hallmark sponsors U.S. and Canadian tour of Winston Churchill's paintings.
	Contemporary Cards are introduced.
1960	Hallmark Foundation is organized.
	Party Goods line is introduced.
1961	First Emmy is presented by National Academy of Television Arts and Sciences to a sponsor — to Joyce C. Hall.
	Playing cards are added to Party line.
	Dwight Eisenhower, in Kansas City at Mr. Hall's invitation for rededication of Liberty Memorial, and Harry Truman end an eight-year feud.
	June 8, Joyce C. Hall is named Honorary Commander of the Order of the British Empire by Her Majesty Queen Elizabeth II.
	December 12, Kansas City Chamber of Commerce presents "Mr. Kansas City" award to Joyce Hall.
1962	Joyce Hall and granddaughter, Libby Marshall, accompany former president Eisenhower to Europe.

Hallmark calendar line makes its debut.

Betsey Clark's "Charmers" are introduced.

1963   Party line is expanded to include party favors.

Joyce Hall receives honorary Doctor of Laws degrees from Kansas State University and the University of Missouri. Later doctorates awarded by Chapman College, 1967; University of Nebraska, 1968; and William Jewell College, 1970.

1964   Hallmark Gallery opens on New York City's fashionable Fifth Avenue and honors Winston Churchill's ninetieth birthday with commemorative exhibit. Hallmark Hall of Fame television presentation, *The Other World of Winston Churchill*, is well received.

A line of Hallmark stationery is introduced.

Hallmark albums become a part of the company's product offering.

1965   Halls Plaza store opens.

Sir Winston Churchill dies and Joyce Hall attends funeral services in London.

1966   Hallmark International is organized as a subsidiary corporation.

Donald J. Hall is named president and chief executive officer of Hallmark Cards, Inc., J.C. Hall continues as chairman of the board.

Hallmark builds new manufacturing center in Topeka.

Lawrence plant is expanded to 450,000 square feet.

Hallmark Candles are introduced.

1967   Crown Center is announced.

Jigsaw puzzles are added to the product line with the acquisition of Springbok.

Hallmark Editions, a library of gift books, is introduced.

1968   Groundbreaking for Crown Center takes place on September 16.

November 4, Rollie B. Hall dies at the age of eighty-six.

A new Leavenworth production center containing 600,000 square feet is built.

Nob Hill Candles are acquired, expanding the existing candle line.

1969   Season inventory and order systems are computerized.

Hallmark Posters are introduced.

Dwight D. Eisenhower dies and Joyce Hall attends private funeral services for him.

1970   Children's Editions are introduced.

A distinctive line of wooden writing instruments is added to the line.

A touring Kaleidoscope program is developed.

1971   J.C. Hall receives the Eisenhower Medallion for international understanding through his work in the People to People program.

October 14, 1971, William F. Hall dies at the age of eighty-seven.

Crown Center office complex is completed.

Hallmark wall plaques are introduced.

Joyce Hall receives the Chancellor Award, Rockhurst College.

1972   The Liberty Distribution Center opens.

Hallmark novelty key chains are introduced.

Midwest Research Institute Citation is awarded to Joyce Hall.

J.C. Hall receives the University of Kansas Distinguished Service Award.

Harry S. Truman dies and Mr. Hall attends private funeral services for him.

1973   First full phase of Crown Center is completed with the opening of the hotel and retail complex.

Halls Crown Center opens.

Hallmark Christmas ornaments are added to the product line.

Sealing wax, picture frames and ceramic figurines are introduced as Hallmark products.

The Hall brothers, William F., born 1884, and Rollie B., born 1882, went into business with Joyce, the youngest, in 1910. This relationship continued for nearly 60 years.

While "W.F." enjoyed office management and inside work, Rollie was the salesman's salesman, devoted to his accounts as they were to him. In his honor, the R. B. Hall medal is given annually to select sales representatives who exemplify the R. B. creed: "He believed that he could succeed only if his customers succeeded, and he sold to them accordingly."

1974   Containers of decorative metal are added to the Hallmark line.

1975   A permanent Kaleidoscope opens in Crown Center.

Trifari, Krussman & Fishel, Inc., makers of "Jewels by Trifari," is acquired.

An Employee Stock Ownership Plan is introduced.

Hallmark is honored by the National Academy of Television Arts and Sciences for twenty-five years of the Hallmark Hall of Fame.

Joyce C. Hall is named "Kansas Citian of the Year" by the Kansas City Press Club on December 18, 1975.

1976   March 15, Elizabeth Ann Dilday Hall, wife of Joyce Hall, dies.

Bath products — soaps, lotion, etc. — are introduced as a new part of the Hallmark line.

Little Gallery debuts as a line of Hallmark gifts.

Costume jewelry, known as "Accents by Hallmark," is test-marketed.

1977   Joyce C. Hall is elected to *Fortune* magazine's Hall of Fame for Business Leadership.

Don Hall is honored in New York by the Parsons School of Design.

Don Hall receives the Chancellor's Medal from the University of Missouri-Kansas City.

Halls Plaza and Swanson's are seriously damaged in a flash flood.

Mutual Benefit Life opens its Western Home Office in Crown Center.

Plans for construction of a Hyatt Regency Hotel in Crown Center are announced.

1978   Sales and Marketing Executives Club of Kansas City honors Don Hall as Kansas City Marketing Executive of the Year.

Hallmark purchases Tandem Jewelry Company.

1979   Plans to build a new Enfield, Connecticut Distribution Center are announced.

Swanson's store is sold to Jack Kaiser, former president of Hallmark Retail Division.

Remodelling of Halls Plaza store begins.

Don Hall named honorary member of American Institute of Architects.

Construction of new parking garage for corporate headquarters begins.

Noon News, a daily publication for employees, celebrates its 25th anniversary, never missing a publication date.

Hallmark Hall of Fame

December 24, 1951	AMAHL AND THE NIGHT VISITORS by Gian Carlo Menotti with *Chet Allen, Andrew McKinley, Rosemary Kuhlmann, Leon Lishner*
April 13, 1952	AMAHL AND THE NIGHT VISITORS *(repeat)*
December 25, 1952	AMAHL AND THE NIGHT VISITORS with *William McIver, Rosemary Kuhlmann*
April 26, 1953	HAMLET by William Shakespeare with *Maurice Evans, Sarah Churchill, Ruth Chatterton, Barry Jones*
December 20, 1953	AMAHL AND THE NIGHT VISITORS *(repeat)*
January 24, 1954	KING RICHARD II by William Shakespeare with *Maurice Evans, Kent Smith, Sarah Churchill*
November 28, 1954	MACBETH by William Shakespeare with *Maurice Evans, Judith Anderson.* EMMY AWARD: Best Actress, *DAME JUDITH ANDERSON.*
December 19, 1954	AMAHL AND THE NIGHT VISITORS *(repeat)*
October 23, 1955	ALICE IN WONDERLAND by Lewis Carroll with *Gillian Barber, Bobby Clark, Eva LeGallienne, Artyne Green, Burr Dillstrom*
November 20, 1955	THE DEVIL'S DISCIPLE by George Bernard Shaw with *Maurice Evans, Teresa Wright, Ralph Bellamy, Dennis King*
December 11, 1955	DREAM GIRL by Elmer Rice with *Vivan Blaine, Hal March*
January 8, 1956	THE CORN IS GREEN by Emlyn Williams with *John Kerr, Eva LeGallienne, Joan Loring, Melville Cooper*
February 5, 1956	THE GOOD FAIRY by Ferenc Molnar with *Julie Harris, Walter Slezak, Cyril Ritchard, Roddy McDowall*
March 18, 1956	THE TAMING OF THE SHREW by William Shakespeare with *Maurice Evans, Lilli Palmer, Diane Cilento*
May 6, 1956	THE CRADLE SONG by Gregorio and Maria Martinez Sierra with *Judith Anderson, Barry Jones, Siobhan McKenna, Anthony Franciosa*
October 28, 1956	BORN YESTERDAY by Garson Kanin with *Mary Martin, Paul Douglas*
November 25, 1956	MAN AND SUPERMAN by George Bernard Shaw with *Maurice Evans, Joan Greenwood*
December 16, 1956	THE LITTLE FOXES by Lillian Hellman with *Greer Garson, Sidney Blackmer, Franchot Tone, E.G. Marshall*
February 10, 1957	THE LARK by Lillian Hellman with *Julie Harris, Eli Wallach, Boris Karloff, Basil Rathbone*
March 15, 1957	THERE SHALL BE NO NIGHT by Robert Sherwood with *Charles Boyer, Katherine Cornell*
April 10, 1957	THE YEOMEN OF THE GUARD by Gilbert and Sullivan with *Alfred Drake, Bill Hayes, Celeste Holm, Barbara Cook*
October 17, 1957	THE GREEN PASTURES by Marc Connelly with *William Warfield, Earl Hyman, Eddie "Rochester" Anderson*
November 17, 1957	ON BORROWED TIME by Paul Osborn with *Ed Wynn, Claude Rains*
December 15, 1957	TWELFTH NIGHT by William Shakespeare with *Maurice Evans*
February 9, 1958	HANS BRINKER by Mary Mapes Dodge with *Tab Hunter, Basil Rathbone, Peggy King, Dick Button*
March 24, 1958	LITTLE MOON OF ALBAN by James Costigan with *Julie Harris, Barry Jones, Christopher Plummer.* George Foster Peabody Award: Outstanding Television Writing, *James Costigan.* EMMY AWARDS: Best Program; Best Direction, *George Schaefer;* Best Writing of a Single Program, *James Costigan;* BEST ACTRESS: *Julie Harris.*

April 25, 1958	DIAL M FOR MURDER by Frederick Knott with *Rosemary Harris, John Williams, Maurice Evans*
October 13, 1958	JOHNNY BELINDA by Elmer Harris with *Julie Harris, Victor Jory, Christopher Plummer, Betty Lou Holland, Rip Torn*
November 20, 1958	KISS ME, KATE by Same and Bella Spewack and Cole Porter with *Alfred Drake, Bill Hayes, Patricia Morison, Harvey Lembeck, Julie Wilson, Jack Klugman.*
December 14, 1958	THE CHRISTMAS TREE by Helen Deutsch with *Ralph Bellamy, Tom Poston, Carol Channing, Cyril Ritchard, Maurice Evans, William Shatner, Hiram Sherman, Jessica Tandy, Margaret Hamilton.*
February 5, 1959	BERKELEY SQUARE by John L. Balderston with *John Kerr, Edna Best, Jeannie Carson, Janet Munro*
March 23, 1959	THE GREEN PASTURES *(repeat)*
April 28, 1959	AH WILDERNESS! by Eugene O'Neill with *Helen Hayes, Burgess Meredith, Lloyd Nolan, Lee Kinsolving, Betty Field*
October 26, 1959	WINTERSET by Maxwell Anderson with *Don Murray, George C. Scott, Piper Laurie, Martin Balsam, Charles Bickford*
November 15, 1959	A DOLL'S HOUSE by Henrik Ibsen with *Julie Harris, Hume Cronyn, Christopher Plummer, Jason Robards, Jr., Eileen Heckart*
December 13, 1959	CHRISTMAS FESTIVAL by Ludwig Bemelmans with *Walter Slezak, Dick Button, Obernkirchen Children's Choir, Judith Anderson, Jules Munshin, Alice Pearce, Hiram Sherman*
February 3, 1960	THE TEMPEST by William Shakespeare with *Maurice Evans, Roddy McDowall, Richard Burton, Lee Remick, Liam Redmond*
April 10, 1960	THE CRADLE SONG by Gregorio and Maria Martinez Sierra with *Helen Hayes, Charles Bickford, Judith Anderson, Geoffrey Horne, Siobhan McKenna, Kathy Willard*
May 2, 1960	CAPTAIN BRASSBOUND'S CONVERSION by George Bernard Shaw with *Christopher Plummer, Greer Garson*
October 25, 1960	SHANGRI-LA by James Hilton with *Richard Basehart, Alice Ghostley, Marisa Pavan, Helen Gallagher, Gene Nelson, Claude Rains*
November 20, 1960	MACBETH by William Shakespeare with *Maurice Evans, Dame Judith Anderson.* EMMY AWARDS: Field of Drama; Single Performance by an Actor, *Maurice Evans;* Single Performance by an Actress, *Dame Judith Anderson;* Program of the Year; Directorial Achievement, *George Schaefer.*
December 16, 1960	GOLDEN CHILD by Paul Engle and Philip Bezanson with *Jerome Hines, Brenda Lewis, Patricia Neway, Stephen Douglass.*
February 7, 1961	TIME REMEMBERED by Jean Anouilh with *Christopher Plummer, Janet Munro, Dame Edith Evans, Barry Jones*
March 26, 1961	GIVE US BARABBAS by Henry Denker with *James Daly, Kim Hunter, Dennis King*
May 5, 1961	THE JOKE AND THE VALLEY by Jerry McNeely with *Dean Stockwell, Keenan Wynn, Thomas Mitchell*
October 20, 1961	MACBETH *(repeat)*
November 30, 1961	VICTORIA REGINA by Laurence Housman with *Julie Harris, Pamela Brown, James Donald, Isabel Jeans, Felix Aylmer, Basil Rathbone*
February 5, 1962	ARSENIC AND OLD LACE by Joseph Kesselring with *Boris Karloff, Mildred Natwick, Tony Randall, Tom Bosley, Dorothy Stickney*
April 15, 1962	GIVE US BARABBAS *(repeat)*
October 26, 1962	THE TEAHOUSE OF THE AUGUST MOON by John Patrick with *John Forsythe, Paul Ford, David Wayne, Miyoshi Umeki*
December 6, 1962	CYRANO DE BERGERAC by Edmond Rostand with *Christopher Plummer, Hope Lange*
February 6, 1963	PYGMALION by George Bernard Shaw with *Julie Harris, John Williams, James Donald, George Rose, Gladys Cooper*
April 4, 1963	THE INVINCIBLE MR. DISRAELI by James Lee with *Trevor Howard,*

266

Greer Garson. EMMY AWARDS: Single Performance by an Actor in a Leading Role, *Trevor Howard;* Electronic Camera Work, *O. Tamburri.*

October 20, 1963   THE TEMPEST *(repeat)*

November 15, 1963   THE PATRIOTS by Sidney Kingsley with *Charlton Heston, John Fraser, Howard St. John, Michael Higgins, Peggy Ann Garner, Frederick O'Neal, Laurinda Barrett*

December 15, 1963   A CRY OF ANGELS by Sherman Yellen with *Walter Slezak, Maureen O'Hara*

February 5, 1964   ABE LINCOLN IN ILLINOIS by Robert Sherwood with *Jason Robards, Jr., Kate Reid*

March 18, 1964   LITTLE MOON OF ALBAN by James Costigan with *Julie Harris, Alan Webb, Dirk Bogarde, Liam Redmond.* EMMY AWARD: Supporting Actress, *Ruth White.*

October 18, 1964   THE FANTASTICKS by Tom Jones and Harvey Schmidt with *Ricardo Montalban, Bert Lahr, Stanley Holloway, Susan Watson, John Davidson*

November 30, 1964   THE OTHER WORLD OF WINSTON CHURCHILL based on "Painting as a Pastime" *Paul Scofield*

December 20, 1964   AMAHL AND THE NIGHT VISITORS by Gian Carlo Menotti with *Martha King, Kurt Yaghijan.* EMMY AWARD: Best Designer, *Warren Clymer* For Hall Of Fame Series.

January 28, 1965   THE MAGNIFICENT YANKEE by Emmet Lavery with *Alfred Lunt, Eduard Franz, Lynn Fontanne, James Daly.* EMMY AWARDS: Program Achievement of the Year; Best Actor, *Alfred Lunt;* Best Actress, *Lynn Fontanne;* Make-Up Artist, *Robert O'Bradovich;* Light Direction, *Phil Hymes.*

April 8, 1965   THE HOLY TERROR by James Lee with *Julie Harris, Brian Bedford, Kate Reid, Alan Webb, Denholm Elliott, Leueen McGrath.* EMMY AWARD: Art Direction and Set Design, *Warren Clymer.*

October 20, 1965   EAGLE IN A CAGE by Millard Lampell with *Trevor Howard, James Daly, Pamela Franklin.* EMMY AWARDS: Supporting Actor, *James Daly;* Writing Achievement in Drama, *Millard Lampell.*

November 18, 1965   INHERIT THE WIND by Jerome Lawrence and Robert E. Lee with *Melvyn Douglas, Ed Begley, Murray Hamilton.* EMMY AWARD: Electronic Production, *O. Tamburri.*

December 12, 1965   AMAHL AND THE NIGHT VISITORS *(repeat)*

February 3, 1966   MAGNIFICENT YANKEE *(repeat)*

April 27, 1966   LAMP AT MIDNIGHT by Barry Stavis with *Melvyn Douglas, Kim Hunter, David Wayne*

November 11, 1966   BAREFOOT IN ATHENS by Maxwell Anderson with *Peter Ustinov, Geraldine Page, Anthony Quayle.* EMMY AWARD, Outstanding Single Performance by an Actor in a Leading Role, *Peter Ustinov*

December 7, 1966   BLITHE SPIRIT by Noel Coward with *Dirk Bogarde, Rachel Roberts, Rosemary Harris*

February 2, 1967   ABE LINCOLN IN ILLINOIS *(repeat)*

March 17, 1967   ANASTASIA by Marcelle Maurett with *Julie Harris, Lynn Fontanne*

April 26, 1967   SOLDIER IN LOVE by Jerome Ross with *Jean Simmons, Claire Bloom, Keith Michell*

November 11, 1967   A BELL FOR ADANO by Paul Osborne with *John Forsythe, Murray Hamilton, Kathleen Widdoes*

December 4, 1967   SAINT JOAN by George Bernard Shaw with *Genevieve Bujold, Maurice Evans, Raymond Massey*

January 31, 1968   ELIZABETH THE QUEEN by Maxwell Anderson with *Dame Judith Anderson, Charlton Heston.* EMMY AWARD: Outstanding Dramatic Program

March 28, 1968   GIVE US BARABBAS *(repeat)*

May 2, 1968   THE ADMIRABLE CRICHTON by James Barrie with *Bill Travers, Virginia McKenna*

November 20, 1968	A PUNT, A PASS AND A PRAYER by David Mark *Hugh O'Brian, Betsy Palmer, Don DeFore*
December 8, 1968	PINOCCHIO by Carlo Collodi *Peter Noone, Burl Ives, Anita Gillette*
February 5, 1969	TEACHER, TEACHER by Allan Sloane *David McCallum, Ossie Davis, Billy Schulman, George Grizzard.* EMMY AWARD: Outstanding Dramatic Television Program; Special Plaque to Billy Schulman
March 28, 1969	GIVE US BARABBAS *(repeat)*
May 2, 1969	VICTORIA REGINA *(repeat)*
November 21, 1969	THE FILE ON DEVLIN by Michael Dyne and Edward Essex *Dame Judith Anderson, Elizabeth Ashley, David McCallum*
December 6, 1969	THE LITTLEST ANGEL by Charles Tazewell *Fred Gwynne, Johnnie Whitaker*
February 6, 1970	A STORM IN SUMMER by Rod Serling with *Peter Ustinov, N'Gai Dixon.* EMMY AWARDS: Dramatic Program; Outstanding Single Performance by an Actor in a Leading Role, *Peter Ustinov.*
March 13, 1970	NEITHER ARE WE ENEMIES by Henry Denker with *Van Heflin, Kate Reid, Ed Begley, Kristoffer Tabori*
May 2, 1970	TEACHER, TEACHER *(repeat)*
November 17, 1970	HAMLET by William Shakespeare with *Richard Chamberlain, Ciaran Madden, Sir Michael Redgrave, Margaret Leighton, Richard Johnson, Sir John Gielgud.* EMMY AWARDS: Supporting Actress, *Margaret Leighton;* Art Direction or Scenic Design, *Peter Roden;* Costume Design, *Martin Baugh and David Walker;* Lighting Direction, *John Rook;* Live or Tape Sound Mixing, *Henry Bird.*
December 6, 1970	THE LITTLEST ANGEL *(repeat)*
February 3, 1971	THE PRICE by Arthur Miller with *George C. Scott, Barry Sullivan, David Burns, Colleen Dewhurst.* EMMY AWARDS: Directorial Achievement, *Fielder Cook;* Outstanding Single Performance by an Actor in a Leading Role, *George C. Scott;* Supporting Actor, *David Burns.* George Foster Peabody Award, Excellence in Dramatic Programming.
March 26, 1971	GIDEON by Paddy Chayefsky with *Peter Ustinov, Jose Ferrer, Arnold Moss, Eric Christmas, Little Egypt.* EMMY AWARD: Lighting Direction, *John Freschi.*
April 27, 1971	A STORM IN SUMMER *(repeat)*
November 15, 1971	THE SNOW GOOSE by Paul Gallico with *Richard Harris, Jenny Agutter.* EMMY AWARD: Supporting Actress, *Jenny Agutter.* George Foster Peabody Award, Dramatic Program Excellence.
December 1, 1971	ALL THE WAY HOME by Tad Mosel with *Joanne Woodward, Richard Kiley, James Woods, Pat Hingle, Eileen Heckart.* George Foster Peabody Award; Dramatic Program Excellence.
December 12, 1971	THE LITTLEST ANGEL *(repeat)*
February 8, 1972	LOVE! LOVE! LOVE! with *Robert Wagner, Bread, Helen Reddy, Mac Davis*
March 22, 1972	HARVEY by Mary Chase with *James Stewart, Helen Hayes, Arlene Francis, Martin Gabel, Fred Gwynne, John McGiver, Richard Mulligan, Jesse White*
May 3, 1972	THE PRICE *(repeat)*
November 17, 1972	THE HANDS OF CORMAC JOYCE by Leonard Wibberly with *Colleen Dewhurst, Stephen Boyd, Dominic Guard*
November 29, 1972	THE MAN WHO CAME TO DINNER by Moss Hart and George S. Kaufman with *Orson Welles, Don Knotts, Lee Remick, Edward Andrews, Joan Collins, Mary Wickes, Peter Haskell, Marty Feldman*
December 12, 1972	THE SNOW GOOSE *(repeat)*
February 9, 1973	YOU'RE A GOOD MAN CHARLIE BROWN by Clark Gesner in collaboration with Charles M. Schulz with *Wendell Burton, Bill*

Hinnant, Ruby Persson, Noelle Matlovsky, Barry Livingston, Mark Montgomery

April 11, 1973 THE SMALL MIRACLE by Paul Gallico with *Raf Vallone, Vittorio De Sica, Marco Della Cava*

November 28, 1973 LISA, BRIGHT AND DARK by John Neufeld with *Anne Baxter, John Forsythe, Kay Lenz*

December 14, 1973 THE BORROWERS by Mary Norton with *Eddie Albert, Tammy Grimes, Dame Judith Anderson, Barnard Hughes, Beatrice Straight.* EMMY AWARDS: Children's Programming, Art Direction, *William Zaharuk;* Set Decoration, *Peter Razmofsky.*

February 5, 1974 THE COUNTRY GIRL by Clifford Odets with *Jason Robards, Shirley Knight Hopkins, George Grizzard*

April 3, 1974 CROWN MATRIMONIAL by Royce Ryton with *Greer Garson, Peter Barkworth, Anna Cropper, Andrew Ray, Amanda Reiss*

November 12, 1974 BRIEF ENCOUNTER by Noel Coward with *Sophia Loren, Richard Burton*

November 29, 1974 THE GATHERING STORM by Sir Winston Churchill with *Richard Burton, Virginia McKenna, Robert Hardy, Ian Bannen*

December 13, 1974 THE BORROWERS *(repeat)*

February 4, 1975 ALL CREATURES GREAT AND SMALL by James Herriot with *Simon Ward, Anthony Hopkins, Lisa Harrow*

March 19, 1975 THE SMALL MIRACLE *(repeat)*

November 10, 1975 ERIC by Doris Lund with *John Savage, Patricia Neal, Claude Akins*

December 3, 1975 VALLEY FORGE by Maxwell Anderson with *Richard Basehart, Victor Barber, Harry Andrews, Simon Ward*

December 12, 1975 THE RIVALRY by Norman Corwin with *Arthur Hill, Charles Durning, Hope Lange*

February 1, 1976 CAESAR AND CLEOPATRA by George Bernard Shaw with *Sir Alec Guiness, Genevieve Bujold*

April 8, 1976 TRUMAN AT POTSDAM by Charles L. Mee, Jr. with *John Houseman, Barry Morse, Jose Ferrer, Ed Flanders*

November 17, 1976 THE DISAPPEARANCE OF AIMEE by John McGreevey with *Bette Davis, William Jordan, Faye Dunaway, James Woods*

December 3, 1976 BEAUTY AND THE BEAST by Sherman Yellen with *George C. Scott, Virginia McKenna, Trish Van Devere, Bernard Lee*

December 12, 1976 PETER PAN by James Barrie with *Danny Kaye, Virginia McKenne, Mia Farrow, Paula Kelly.* EMMY AWARD: Animation, *Jean Dejoux and Elizabeth Savel.*

February 7, 1977 EMILY, EMILY by Allan Sloane with *John Forsythe, Pamela Bellwood, Thomas Hulce, James Farentino, Karen Grassle*

March 29, 1977 ALL CREATURES GREAT AND SMALL *(repeat)*

November 16, 1977 THE LAST HURRAH by Edwin O'Connor with *Carroll O'Connor, Mariette Hartley, Patrick Wayne, Kitty Winn, Dana Andrews, Jack Carter, Burgess Meredith, Patrick O'Neal*

December 1, 1977 THE COURT-MARTIAL OF GEORGE ARMSTRONG CUSTER by Douglas C. Jones with *Brian Keith, Blythe Danner, James Olson, Ken Howard, Susan Sullivan, Stephen Elliott*

December 16, 1977 HAVE I GOT A CHRISTMAS FOR YOU by Jerome Coopersmith with *Milton Berle, Sheree North, Harold Gould, Alex Cord, Adrienne Barbeau, Jayne Meadows, Jack Carter, Jim Backus, Steve Allen*

February 2, 1978 "TAXI!!!" by Lanford Wilson with *Eva Marie Saint, Martin Sheen*

March 16, 1978 PETER PAN *(repeat)*

November 17, 1978 RETURN ENGAGEMENT with *Elizabeth Taylor, Joseph Bottoms*

November 30, 1978 FAME with *Richard Benjamin, Jose Ferrer, Raf Vallone*

December 17, 1978 STUBBY PRINGLE'S CHRISTMAS with *Beau Bridges, Julie Harris*

April 6, 1979 BEAUTY AND THE BEAST *(repeat)*

PHOTO CREDITS AND SOURCES OF HISTORICAL PRINTS: Lou Charno: Title page. Nebraska State Historical Society: 12; 28 (top). Historical Collection of the Union Pacific Railroad: 13 (bottom). Norfolk, Nebraska, Historical Society: 13 (top). Missouri Valley Room, Kansas City, Missouri, Public Library: 28 (bottom); 33; 40 (top and bottom); 41; 43 (top); 48 (top and center); 49; 50 (center). Kansas City Museum of History and Science: 43 (bottom); 48 (bottom); 50 (bottom left and bottom right); 51 (all photos). Private collection of Fred Wolferman: 50 (top). Karsh, Ottawa: 79 (top left). Paul Kivett: 89 (bottom); 184 (bottom). Fred Kautt: 124 (number 19). Ted Spiegel: 124 (number 20); 125 (numbers 17 and 18). Life Magazine photo by Bob Peterson: 142 (center right and bottom); 143. Henry Groskinsky: 252.

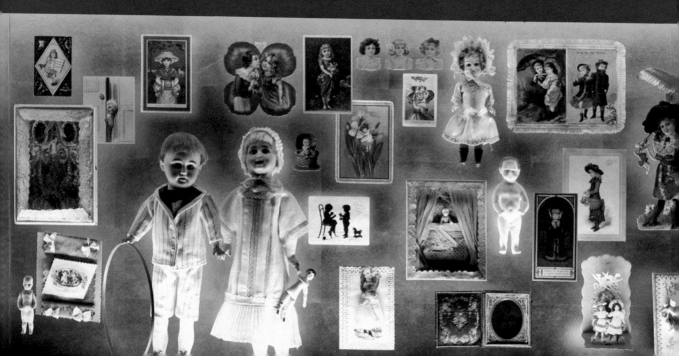

ACKNOWLEDGEMENTS: Disney material contained herein: © Walt Disney Productions: 158 and 159. *Saturday Evening Post*: 163 (top). Grandma Moses: "Sugaring Off," © 1946 by Dryden Press, Inc., copyright © renewed 1974 by Otto Kallir, assigned 1974 to Grandma Moses Properties, Inc.: 163 (bottom). Peanuts material: © United Feature Syndicate, Inc.: 186. Saul Steinberg material used by his permission: 195 and 196. "A Friend's Greeting" from *A Heap O'Livin'* by Edgar A. Guest. Copyright 1916. Reprinted by permission of Reilly & Lee, a division of Henry Regnery Company: 198. Excerpt from *A Third Treasury of Kahlil Gibran*. Copyright © 1975, 1973, 1966, 1965 by Philosophical Library, Inc. Reprinted by permission of the publisher, Citadel Press: 199. Excerpt from *The Open Door* by Helen Keller. Copyright © 1957 by Helen Keller. Reprinted by permission of Doubleday & Company, Inc.: 199.

A three dimensional history of greeting cards created by Alexander Girard.